Whispers of Betrayal

BLACK WOMEN IN CRISIS

Jefferey McGill

authorHOUSE®

AuthorHouse™
1663 Liberty Drive
Bloomington, IN 47403
www.authorhouse.com
Phone: 1-800-839-8640

First published by AuthorHouse   10/24/2011

ISBN: 978-1-4567-2516-7 (sc)
ISBN: 978-1-4567-2514-3 (hc)
ISBN: 978-1-4567-2515-0 (ebk)

Library of Congress Control Number: 2011900818

Printed in the United States of America

Dedication

"*Whispers of Betrayal: Black Women in Crisis*" is dedicated to the growing ranks of single black women fighting to gain respect and survive in a society that has traditionally been very hostile to them. Sadly, black women are fighting for respect without united support from a growing number of black men who seem more interested in seeking pleasure, security, and acceptance from women of other races.

I dedicate "*Whispers of Betrayal Black Women in Crisis*" to all black women but especially to Saartjie (Sara) Baartman, an African woman who was dehumanized, exploited and disrespected by English and French people during the early nineteenth century, when England and France represented Europe's greatest powers. I discuss her life in chapter 1. Even though Saartjie (Sara) Baartman's physical build is not representative of all black women, Europeans took her anatomy and with a broad brush painted an unflattering picture of bestiality for women of African descent.

In order to know the truth, one must love the truth.

Forever Bound

Life is an unrelenting moment to moment express a sublimating journey that begins with an intense spiritual yearning that drives us through matrixes of the imagination. The forever bound express of life pauses briefly at junctures of change and then moves on along rails of expectation to realities beyond our wildest dreams.

Jeff McGill

"A consciousness of wrongdoing is the first step to salvation." This remark of Epicurus is a very good one. For a person who is not aware that he or she is doing anything wrong has no desire to put it right. You have to catch yourself doing it before you can reform. Some people boast about their failings; can you imagine someone, who counts faults as merits, ever giving thought to their cure? So, to the best of your ability, demonstrate your own guilt, conduct inquiries of your own into all evidence against yourself. Play the part of the prosecutor, then of the judge, and finally of pleader in mitigations of your actions. Be harsh with yourself at times."

Seneca

Contents

Introduction

"Whispers of Betrayal Black Women in Crisis" is written to caution black men of the dangers of betraying black women for women of other races. The problem is much greater than that; however black men choosing women of other races over black women exhibit utter confusion. A black man's growing interest in replacing black women as his mate while channeling his resources to women of other races is an act of complicity in the decimation of communities of color and it also signals a dangerous lapse of reason on the part of black men of a relentless assault on the freedom and privileges of black people by the criminal justice system.

Divided by different priorities, the problems created by this disconnect between black men and black women will lead to dire consequences for black men who are being stealthily disenfranchised by a biased criminal justice system that hand them felony convictions and permanently placing them in a lower caste in society. Black women are black men's greatest source of resilience, strength, and salvation but in periods of prosperity, many black men have lost perspective of the significance of black women to his very existence.

Even though I take on a very sensitive issue, I do not want those white persons, for whom the shoe does not fit to feel they have been thrown under the bus. There are good and evil people in every race. Certainly not all white people are evil. Whites and blacks are being pitted against each other while a small 1 or 2 percent of wealthy white men are architects of plans to deprive black men of their freedom as a social under caste by disease, mass incarceration and felony disenfranchisement through the war on drugs.

Unfortunately and unwittingly, many innocent and virtuous whites stand idle as the life, liberty, and pursuit of happiness is denied on a massive scale to young black men via felony convictions. In this injustice, American society perpetrates betrayal of black women by locking available black men into inferior positions because of a felony record. In the criminalization of black men as felons, they are discriminated against for employment and housing, and denied the right to vote, educational opportunities, food stamps, inclusion on juries, and other benefits.

As long as unjust forms of government are destructive to so many black Americans, it is the right for a silent majority of whites to alter or abolish the injustice of mass incarceration, and to institute new government that is for equality and justice for all Americans. The danger of the majority going along with depriving blacks of their rights is that theirs rights and entitlements are being eroded as well. Blacks are like the canaries in the coal mine: what kills them will ultimately spread to others in society.

There are people like the late Boyd Graves who insist that the AIDS virus was created in laboratories. Statistics from the Joint United Nations Programme on HIV/AIDS (UNAIDS) report over 27 million deaths worldwide by HIV/AIDS since 1991. The death toll in Africa from AIDS was 1.4 million in 2008 and 1.3 million in 2009. Although Africa is inhabited by just over 14.7 percent of the world's population, it is estimated to have more than 88 percent of people living with HIV and 92 percent of all AIDS deaths in 2007. (UNAIDS) has predicted outcomes for the region to the year 2025. These range from a plateau and eventual decline in deaths beginning around 2012 to a catastrophic continual growth in the death rate with potentially 90 million cases of infection.

Boyd Graves a lawyer and 1975 graduate of the US Naval Academy discovered he was HIV positive. Rather than lie down and accept it as a death sentence, he resolved to learn all he could about the disease in hopes of seeking a cure. What Graves discovered shocked and enraged him. Based on information he discovered in the public domain and through the Freedom of Information Act, he concluded the US government was involved in a super secret Special Virus Cancer Program he felt was the cause of the dreaded disease HIV/AIDS.

In 1999, Graves discovered the secret 1971 *Special Virus Cancer Flow Chart,* which spells out the incremental development of a laboratory-produced virus designed to attack and undermine the immune systems of people of African descent. Graves sought support from various government agencies, including, the General Accounting Office, former Ohio congressman James Traficant, AIDS organizations, and the courts.

Graves sued the US government in Federal Court in San Diego California in an attempt to get it to confess to its role in the creation of HIV/AIDS. If Mr. Graves's assertion that HIV/AIDS was produced in US labs is true, the life and liberty of all people of color are seriously threatened.

Michelle Alexander emphatically states that mass incarceration is a new form of social control design to perpetuate racial caste in America. Black people have not ended racial castes in America. She writes extensively in "*The New Jim Crow*" about how the criminal justice system of the United States is being used as a tool for social control using mass incarceration of young black men with felony records to create an under caste in society without the right to vote, and without equal opportunities to be employed. "Racial caste" denotes a stigmatized racial group locked into an inferior position by law and customs. Jim Crow and slavery were caste systems and so are the objectives of mass incarcerations by the current criminal justice system. Michelle Alexander states:

> As the United States celebrates the nation's "triumph over race," with the election of Barack Obama, the majority of young black men in major American cities are locked behind bars or labeled felons for life. Jim Crow laws were wiped off the books decades ago, but today an astounding percentage of the African American community is warehoused in prisons or trapped in a permanent, second-class status-much like their grandparents before them, who lived under an explicit system of control.

In her work, keys are provided to unlock doors that lead to freedom for black men. Those keys are knowledge of a plan to make black men a permanent member of an under caste society.

Alexander points out that mass incarceration refers not only to the criminal justice system but also to the larger web of laws, rules, policies, and customs that control black men labeled as criminals both in and out of prison. Once released, former black prisoners enter a hidden underworld of legalized discrimination and permanent social exclusion. Black men become members of America's new under caste.

Once black males with a felony record become members of society's under caste, they cannot move up in society, as they are locked out of mainstream society and economy. Many turn to street hustles as pimps and drug dealers, and live a life of violence and crime. Some capitalize on these experiences as rappers. Hip-hop lyrics are testimonials to the trials and tribulations of the life of the under caste in society and their struggle to make money on the perimeters of society.

With HIV and mass incarceration of blacks, it is not a stretch to say there are plans to destroy—through disease, mass incarceration, and the justice systems—the life and livelihood of black people. Chancellor Williams, author of "*Destruction of Black Civilization Great Issues of a Race from 4500 B.C. to 2000 A.D*" stated "white people are the implacable foe, the traditional and everlasting enemy of black people." There is perpetual covert struggle between blacks and whites centered on whites feeling they are superior to blacks.

Chancellor William's viewpoint appears not to be farfetched for anyone who dares make an honest assessment of historical and contemporary treatment of dark-skinned blacks throughout African and American societies by the great colonial empires who have enslaved black people and confiscated untold resources in Africa. Proof of double standards in Africa is the practice of apartheid in South Africa; proof of double standards in America starts with the framers of the Constitutions. Their contradictory actions are shown in the stated belief that all men were created equal. One wonders at what truth they held that permitted black people to be enslaved like animals or what truths are being held today as self evident that all men are created equal, as the justice system incarcerates under felony convictions, massive numbers of young black men.

More than one in four U.S. presidents were slaveholder: twelve owned slaves at some point in their lives. Significantly, eight presidents owned slaves while living in the Executive Mansion. Put another way, for fifty of the first sixty years of the new republic, the president was a slaveholder.

Following is the number of slaves owned by each of the twelve slaveholding presidents. (Names in all caps indicate the president owned slaves while serving as the chief executive.)

- GEORGE WASHINGTON (two hundred fifty to three hundred)
- THOMAS JEFFERSON (two hundred)
- JAMES MADISON (one hundred)
- JAMES MONROE (seventy five)
- ANDREW JACKSON (two hundred)
- Martin Van Buren (one)
- William Henry Harrison (eleven)
- JOHN TYLER (seventy)
- JAMES POLK (twenty five)
- ZACHARY TAYLOR (one hundred fifty)
- Andrew Johnson (probably eight)
- Ulysses S. Grant (probably five)

It's a common belief that Abraham Lincoln never trafficked in slaves, much less owned them; indeed, he "freed the slaves." But here's the shocker: although the slave trade had been abolished in the District of Columbia in 1850, slaves inhabited the capital for another fifteen years till the end of the Civil War. Dwell on that thought: Lincoln fought the Civil War in a slave city; the Great Emancipator inhabited a White House staffed by slaves.

Our earliest presidents struggled to find solutions. The most radical proposal in the early days of the republic was to ship slaves and other blacks back to Africa. Jefferson was keen on the idea, believing that blacks would eventually have to be removed from the United States or whites would live in perpetual dread that the slaves would rise up in rebellion. Such fears prompted a later president, James Monroe, to support the creation of the Society for the Colonization of Free People of Color of America, better known as the American Colonization Society in 1816.

The society was not just well-intentioned. It raised money, acquired lands in what is present-day Liberia, and supported passage of emancipated slaves, former indentured servants, and free blacks across the Atlantic to the west coast of Africa. The society named the major settlement in the colony Monrovia in honor of our nation's fifth president.

Blacks have been very useful to white men as a source of free labor in the theft of gold and diamonds from the people of Africa and building wealth for whites in America's agricultural enterprises. As Martin Luther King stated:

> Blacks, and all other non-white people, were to be the burden bearers for the real citizens of this nation. Martin Luther King Jr., speech to the Montgomery Improvement Association (5 December 1955)

After slaves were emancipated, thoughts of shipping blacks back to Africa was considered a better solution to managing the black problem, rather than integrating blacks into society.

Black people have come a long way, but their problems are far from being over, as racism and bigotry still provide formidable obstacles. This is no time for black men to lose their mind on sexual whims. Black men forgetting their history and turning their backs on methods of population control such as slavery, Jim Crow, and mass incarceration of their own kind while turning away from black women for women of other races are critically missing in action for the challenge ahead for black people. Black women have always had to deal with the betrayal by institutional policies such as slavery, Jim Crow, and now mass incarceration of black men. Black women are now forced to deal with the outright betrayal caused by black men's escalating interest in women of other races.

Until policies of mass incarceration of blacks end and antiretroviral medicines are free and available to end the death count of millions of

Africans and black Americans a year, it is not a stretch to continue to state that a small minority of white men controlling wealth and the government are their bitter enemies.

Eugene Robinson in "*Disintegration the Splintering of Black America*," asserts that the African American population in the United States has always been seen as a single entity: a "black America" with unified interests and needs. Robinson argues that over decades of desegregation, affirmative action, and immigration, the concept of black America has shattered. Instead of one black America, now there are four:

- A mainstream middle-class with a full ownership stake in American society.
- A large abandoned minority with less hope of escaping poverty and dysfunction than at any time since Reconstruction's crushing end.
- A small transcendent elite with such enormous wealth, power, and influence that even white folks have to genuflect.
- And two newly emergent groups—individuals of mixed-race and communities of recent black immigrants—that makes us wonder what "black" is even supposed to mean.

The splintering of one black America into four makes unity of blacks almost impossible. Each splintered group has its own cares, challenges and concerns. They view each other with mistrust and apprehension. Adding to that is the complication created when black men turn away from black women for women of other races.

Unity among blacks has been prevented for so many centuries that the various mechanisms to keep blacks disorganized have been perfected in the Western system of control. Slavery was replaced by Jim Crow and now Jim Crow has been made over by the new approach of mass incarceration with felony records that ensure the subordinate status of blacks

I have no problem with successful, wealthy grown black men choosing women of other races as a lifelong mate. Just because we have a black president, we still have not overcome racial prejudice, and because women of other races now accept a wealthy black man as a caretaker and provider does not equate to race-neutral status in America. There are many more issues black men and women must resolve together if black people are to survive what seems to be a curse of dark skin in Caucasian societies. Black men please increase your awareness of the crisis being faced by black women and ultimately the challenge on hand for the survival of black people from the ravages of HIV/AIDS and mass incarceration. Black people are truly an endangered species.

Under socio economic pressures and, physical and psychological stress, black men have lost the ability to be vigilant about the best interest of self and black women. He is lost in the bowels of a Leviathan. Locked within the bowels of this Leviathan called America, black men's betrayal of self and black women has almost reached fruition.

CHAPTER I

The Ongoing Struggle of Black Women for Redemption

Africans using less-advanced weapons against guns and cannons, were hunted, captured, and enslaved. Once defeated, black men could do very little to protect black women and children from a harsh fate of servitude and death for many.

Today, there are no excuses for black men not to protect black women. Black women were vulnerable in the early nineteenth century, many black women of today are just as vulnerable facing economic hardships alone and fighting depression.

In the bounds of slavery black women and black men had few rights and were treated with the same regard as animals. Like a cow or a horse, the owners of slaves exercised unlimited power to force submission to their will. Black women and their children did not enjoy the normal social structure of social bonds that fostered personal development that promoted mental health. Black women were expected to work like an ox.

The only time she had to care for her children was late night and early mornings after back breaking work in the fields for more than sixteen

1

hours. Black women prepared food from discarded parts of animals the slave owner found unfit to eat. Her squalid dwelling was cold with nothing but dirt floor. Black women not only raised her children but also cared for the children of female and male slaves sold away to other plantations. Ultimately, black women had to come to grips with the pain of watching her children sold off as well. The mixed blood of thousands upon thousands of African peoples' descendants is incontrovertible proof of sexual contact between white slave masters and black slave women.

The State Law Partus Sequitur Ventrem intended all children born of enslaved black women would be slaves forever. White men were motivated to rape black women for sexual pleasure and they also forced black male slaves to impregnate them. Black women were bred like animals and their offspring sold for profit.

It took tremendous strength and resolve for black women to survive such wanton misuse and abuse. There is extensive documentation in slave narratives of the heartless rape and sexual coercion endured by black women. What must it have been like for male African slaves, as they lay on the squalid tenements floors of slave shacks, to hear the agonizing screams of black women being tortured, beaten, and sexually abused through the night?

For very minor offenses, and many times her refusal to have sex with white men, black women were often hung by their wrists, stripped naked, and beaten with whips until their flesh was laid open.

Even pregnant black women were shown very little mercy. There are accounts in slave narratives of pregnant black women beaten into miscarriages and dying from severe beatings. Even though this physical trauma happened to her ancestors, today's black woman is reminded each day of the psychological trauma endured by her ancestors through her second-class status to white women in the media, most glaringly in the fashion and modeling industries, and in the movie industries.

It was no crime if white men robbed black women of their virtue. Yet it was heinous if a black man was caught with a white prostitute. If a black man was caught with any type of white woman, prostitute or not, he was tortured and killed.

The rape of black women was always explained away or excused with the contention that sex took place because black women instigated the rape through their natural uncontrollable, animal like cravings, rather than because of the unrestrained desires of white men. Black female slaves lived in constant fear that her man or children would be sold away if she did not give in to sexual advances. The psychological traumas of such an existence should not be underestimated. Its continuity from slavery to the present day should not be discounted as that was then and it has no impact today.

To the people who have it in their history, the legacy of slavery is a discounting heritage. The ravages inflicted during slavery remains damaging to the development of family instinct of the black community. For black people, the legacy of slavery has forged emphasis on being individuals and not families, development in the black community of shelters and not homes, living in herds, like animals devoid of family values that are cultivated through marriages. How unfortunate for blacks in America to have such psychological trauma heaped upon them as slaves and then to be given their freedom in such psychological disarray then expected to tie together and strengthen the scattered loose ends of broken spirits. At the same time, they were expected to establish roots and develop bonds of love with a dysfunctional and battered psyche.

At the onset of their freedom from slavery, black women were without protection or financial resources. It was open season on blacks by members of the Ku Klux Klan. Black women, although free, found themselves still dependent on white men and white women for their survival.

Much like black men in prison today on felonies, freed slaves were limited by black codes from finding work, joining the military, voting or serving on juries to testify against whites who committed crimes against blacks. Black were limited as to where and how they could travel. They needed permits to congregate in large groups and were forced into contract labor if they were unwilling to work for proposed wages.

Jim Crow denied black men access to white women yet offered little protection for black women working on the properties of white men or against white men in the courts of law. It was a punishable offense for

Negroes to travel with, eat with, defecate in the same facility as, be buried with, make love with, play with, relax with, or even talk to whites except in the context of master-and-servant interaction.

The environment in the North was not as overtly racist as the South, but blacks privileges were only slightly less restrained than in the South. Under the weight of such discriminative practices, black women-though now free-did not blink in their efforts to transmit belief, pride and values to their children. Again, like in the slave quarters, she took on the lead role in organizing family life, making a home in the shabbiest of habitats, and fighting to educate her children, all while working backbreaking jobs.

The black woman and her family continue to be impacted negatively by high rates of unemployment. Many of the gains made by blacks in the 1960's have been lost as immigrants of the United States from other nations are awarded favored status. After enduring all of this hardship, at the forefront of harm to black women today is the callous disrespect on many levels dished out to them by a growing rank of successful black men.

Since the murder of Martin Luther King, there are very few fierce leaders among the ranks of black men, who are adamant about protecting black women, young and old. Black women continue to fight the good fight of holding onto their dignity. Black men's strength, will, and wisdom are vital support structures for black women and vital to the stability of black families throughout the world.

Statistics inform us that black women are fighting a losing battle. Instead of jumping the broom, black men in increasing numbers are jumping ship entirely and leaving black women with very few upwardly mobile black men in the dating pool. Interracial dating and intermarriage have increased in the last century due to greater human mobility via transportation and multicultural expanding demographics via immigration.

Today, in America 6 percent of marriages are interracial; in 1970, it was less than 1percent. A Gallup Poll on interracial dating in June 2005 reported that 95 percent of eighteen- to twenty-nine-year-olds approve of blacks and whites dating. About 60 percent of that age group said they have dated someone of a different race.

In the Southern states, there remains a widespread public perception among whites that predatory black men cannot resist a desire for sex with white women. Black men have been lynched for whistling at white women. In one famous case, a fourteen year-old black boy named Emmett Till, whistled at a white woman and, was murdered by Mississippi Klansmen in 1955.

In 1970 there were only sixty-five thousand marriages involving African-Americans and whites. Interracial marriages have tripled since 1970, and black-unions have quadrupled in the past twenty years. Out of 1.3 million interracial marriages, 260,000 are black-white and 171,000 are between black men and white women. In 2005, that number had grown to 422,000. Among all interracial couples, they represented two percent of marriages in 1970 according to data compiled in a Stanford University study by Michael Rosenfeld. In 2005, that number was up to seven percent of the 59 million marriages in the United States. The statistics, however, do not reflect the increasing number of interracial couples who are dating or living together.

In 1990, nearly 8 percent of all married black men between the ages of twenty-five and thirty-four, married nonblack women; 4 percent of white men in the same age category married outside their race.

In the Pacific Northwest, 32 percent of black men marry white women; in California, 22 percent; in the Rocky Mountain region 30 percent; and in the New England states, 19 percent of black men marry white women. Overall, more than two hundred thousand black men are married outside their race, mostly to white women. That means there are two hundred thousand black women who very well could be in stable productive relationships with black men who are not.

The 2000 US Census confirms many black women's complaint that black men choose women of other races far more than white men. For this to be true, white women are far more embracing of black men than white men are interested in black women. Six percent of all black husbands are in interracial marriages. Two percent of black wives are in interracial relationships. The percentage of black men cohabitating with white women is much higher at 14 percent. Black women cohabitating with white men is significantly less at 3 percent.

African American men married white women 2.65 times more than African American women married white men. In 73 percent of black-white marriages, the husband was black. The percentage is even higher in relationship where couples are just cohabitating. Black men live with women of other races five times more than black women live with men of other races. Because of black men's choice of women of other races, the house of the African American family is falling down.

In her article "Black Men White Women: What's the Furor" (Ebony, Nov 1994), Lynn Norment suggests the problem presented for black women by black men interracial interest.

Black women find the choices of wives for prominent pro athletes increasingly frustrating. O.J. Simpson, Tiki Barber, Barry Bonds, Tiger Woods, and a host of other athletes continue to allow women of other races to benefit from their blessings of wealth and fame. O.J. Simpson eventually lost everything; Barry Bonds was ordered to pay his ex-wife $30,000 a month; it is reported that Tiger paid hundreds of millions in divorce settlements; and Tiki Barber's life is in disarray, bouncing between one interracial relationship to another. All marriages have challenges. It becomes particularly unsettling when black men turn away from black women to fail in relationships with white women and end up enriching white families that already have financial security. There is so much controversy over the actions of many prominent and even not-so-prominent black men. Opposition to the increasing choices of black men selecting lifestyles with women of other races, is as strong as ever in both black and white communities.

Although many high-profile black men are married to black women, there are so many more who choose women of other races that these choices of women of other races, in the minds of many black women, is at epidemic proportion. There are not enough eligible black men for black women to share. The shortage for college-educated black women becomes even more glaring in view of how many black men are college-educated.

Dr. Halford Fairchild, an associate professor of psychology and Black Studies at Pitzer College in Claremont, California states in Ebony article, Nov 1994, "Black Men/White Women," that:

> Black man—white woman relationship is a recurring theme and source of friction a among black female college students . . . Black men are underrepresented on campuses and in the profession . . . The rarity makes them a hot commodity and they are sought after by both black women and non black women.

Dr Fairchild further states, "Many black women find themselves without sexual partners . . . Many are sexually frustrated, compounding other chronic problems in their lives . . . When they see a black man with a white woman, it symbolizes all of the problems they are experiencing and creates resentment."

Studies reports there are thirty-five to forty-five single black men who are in college or have jobs for every one hundred black women. Hundreds of thousands of black men are imprisoned and high numbers of black men are felons whose lives are interlaced with crimes and drugs.

Statistically black men become increasingly unavailable to college educated black women. Pro athletes, well-educated, and well-employed black men, such as Tiki Barber, Michael Strahan, Tiger Woods, Charles Barkley, Kobe Bryant, Lamar Odoms, Frank Thomas, Scottie Pippen, Ice Tea, Al Jarreau, Tim Duncan, Lionel Richie, Montel William, Clarence Thomas, Quincy Jones, Sidney Potier, and Seal are married to women of other races.

As the dating pool for a black woman shrinks, she is left to struggle alone, in many instances a single head of household with children. The median income for black households was $34,218 in 2008, the lowest of any group. A single black woman with children had a median annual

income of $25,958 in 2008. "One in five black families live in poverty."
Four out of ten black families headed by a single mother are poor.

While 50 percent of all Americans were married in 2008, the figure for
blacks was 30%, despite nearly identical divorce rates. 47 percent of black
Americans have never been married, versus 30 percent of whites. 45.3
percent of black women have never been married, versus 28 percent of
white women. 29.3 percent of black households with children are headed
by a single woman, versus 12.5 percent for white households. 13.2 percent
of black households with children are headed by a married couple, versus
21.4 percent for white households.

Black women confronted with increasing costs of mortgages, rent,
groceries, and insurance, have no income left for savings for college, health
matters and emergencies. She alone cannot prepare her children for success
in a competitive society. As black kids are less-able to afford college, they
fall behind in the ability to amass wealth and are recycled in the poverty
loop. Single female-headed households are more likely than those of other
races of women to remain in that cycle of poverty. In 2008, the poverty
rate for black households with children was 28.2 percent (versus 14.9
percent for whites.)

- The poverty rate for single female-headed black households with
  children was 42.1percent
- The poverty rate for married-parent black households with
  children was 8.3 percent.

Black women are waiting longer to walk down the aisle. By the time
some get there, they have already had one or two children. If the children
are by different fathers, these women's lives are further complicated.

How disappointing is it for black mothers to observe black sons
turning against their black daughters? Because of the growing preference
of black men for women of other races, black women are forced, in many
cases, to add men of other races to their dating pool or not date at all.

The trends and choices of contemporary black men are very disturbing
to black women. It is also disturbing to black males such as myself to see the

shameful and disrespectful actions of prospering black males who dismiss black women. It makes me think of the hardship my mother endured as a single parent. The black men of her times may have been uneducated and ignorant of the damage they were doing to their women. The same cannot be said for the betrayal of black women by black men of today.

Martin Luther King Jr. had a dream that black people would overcome racial injustice. For the most part, his dream has been realized. Today, black men, standing high on the shoulders of Martin Luther King and freedom fighters, have unfinished business. Many of the black men choosing women of other races for wives seek the blessing of their activity from black women still struggling to overcome social bias and discrimination in America. In many circumstances, black women become the bridesmaids of the many white women who marry the crème de la crème of black men. How insulting is that for many black women?

I would like to propose an analogy. Take a man who deserts his family and start another family. The family he deserted is impoverished and struggles to survive (single black women and single black women head of household); the second family (women of other races) is prospering and very well cared for. This is what it is like for black women. Black men are deserting black women, his first obligation, for women of other races. It is not the interracial relationship that I vent at. It is the neglect of black men of black women that is problematic for me.

On the surface, most will say a man's choice is his own and no one should choose for him. If black women were taken care of and not struggling for a mate, I could understand the interest in women of other races. Black men have unfinished business with Martin Luther King Jr's dream. Black men and women suffered racial oppression together and should help each other overcome the institutional stumbling blocks still prevalent for black people in society. Black men should take pride in themselves and black women like true African warriors. I write this book to remind them.

CHAPTER 2

Who Is Saartjie (Sara) Baartman? Ties of Racial Insensitivity to European Culture

Cultural and social norms in Europe have a trickle-down influence on American values and mores. European ideas about black women were forged by the physique of one black woman Saartjie Baartman. Saartjie Baartman (1789-1816) was born during the period of Dutch colonization in South Africa. Her indigenous name is uncertain, but the name Saartjie is Dutch for "little Sara." Baartman was raised in a rural indigenous community of Khoisan, the descendants of the Khoi Khoi people (who were rumored to have been wiped out during her time period).

The Khoikhoi ("people people" or "real people") or Khoi, in standardized Khoekhoe/Nama orthography spelled Khoekhoe, are a historical division of the Khoisan ethnic group, the native people of southwestern Africa, and closely related to the Bushmen (or San, as the Khoikhoi called them). They had lived in southern Africa since the fifth century. When European immigrants colonized the area in 1652, the Khoi Khoi were practicing extensive pastoral agriculture in the Cape region, with large herds of Nguni cattle. The European immigrants labeled them Hottentots, in imitation of the sound of the Khoisan languages, but this term is now considered derogatory.

11

Both the Khoi Khoi and San were thought of as the missing link between humans and apes because of their hunter-gatherer lifestyles and unusual speech patterns. Europeans dehumanized the Khoi Khoi and San, using such racist views to eliminate the native people from resource-rich land, where diamonds and gold were found.

Baartman was a married woman. During raids of extermination she lost her husband and family. Eventually she migrated to the urban center of Cape Town for survival, where she worked as a slave to a Boer farmer named Peter Cezar. Hendrik Cezar, the brother of Peter Cezar, first noticed Baartman during a visit to the house and later conceived of the "Hottentot Venus" show during his visit.

The show, which was to take place in London, would exploit European interests in African natives, especially in the "Hottentots." The Hottentot Venus show would also capitalize on the European obsession in so-called primitive sexuality, described in the tall-tale accounts of explorers who fabricated stories of "Hottentot" women's oversized buttocks and mysterious apron-like flap of skin covering their vaginal area. Hendrik Cezar convinced Baartman to enter into a contract for the "Hottentot Venus" show, in which she would share in the profits of her exhibition.

Saartjie Baartman was not college educated. After losing her husband and family in raids on her village by slave traders, Saartjie had suffered great trauma in her life. Alone and fearful, she eventually agreed to leave her home for a cold and inhospitable environment in Europe to be paraded around like an animal. She arrived in London in September 1810. Cezar advertised the show and billed Baartman as a "most correct specimen of her race."

The "Hottentot Venus" exhibition was instantly popular and inspired political cartoons, thus demonstrating how the icon of the Hottentot Venus became a fixture in the culture. Cartoon images created a fetish out of Saartjie Baartman's backside. The cartoons served as the basis for the fashion development of the bustle. The mid-to-late-nineteenth-century bustle gave the illusion of a large bottom.

The mistreatment and exploitation of Saartjie created outrage, as complaints about seeing her in a cage infuriated some individuals. It seemed Baartman was forced to appear nearly nude under threats of violence by her exhibitor. Hendrik Cezar was eventually brought to trial under charges of forcing Saartjie into slavery and public indecency.

Baartman testified but did not corroborate stories of being held against her will. She only complained about not having enough clothes to wear. The courts dismissed the case only mandating that Cezar cease and desist the indecency. As a result, the show disappeared into the less-scrutinized English countryside. In 1814, Cezar and Baartman surfaced in Paris, where Cezar sold Saartjie to an animal trainer named Reaux. The "Hottentot Venus" show caused the same sensation in Paris as it had in London.

Saartjie was exhibited as a freak affirming white's ideals of their superiority and using Saartjie to affirm ideas of bestial sexuality of black women. Prancing in the nude, with her large buttocks and extraordinary clitoral development, Saartjie provided the foundation for racist and pseudo-scientific theories about black inferiority, being closer to Apes than humans, and black female sexuality. Audiences in London and Paris found Saartjie Baartman's steatopygia (protruding buttocks) particularly fascinating, as the "proved" medical/anthropological ideas during of the time about the sexual lasciviousness and animality of African women.

Africans and other supposedly inferior groups, such as the Irish, Indians, Maoris, and women, all displayed, it was held, childlike characteristics. The *Saturday Review* of September 8, 1866 referred to the Indian as "childish and impulsive," the term "impulsive" referring to lack of weighed and considered thought. Similarly, Francis Galton's "Hereditary Talent and Character," in the 1865 *Macmillan's* magazine argued "the Negro has strong impulsive habits, and neither patience, reticence, nor dignity."

The physiology of Baartman attracted the attention of natural scientists, including George Cuvier. In March 1815, Baartman now was an alcoholic and subjected to scientific observations. The scientists enticed her with alcohol and sweets to pose nude. Baartman refused to reveal what they had hoped to witness: a view of her clitoris.

When Baartman died from complications of alcoholism, Cuvier acquired her cadaver, using it to write his 1817 scientific thesis that unveiled the mystery of her "apron." Cuvier compared her genitalia with those of apes and crafted racist scientific theories, which circulated for more than a century, on African women's oversexed and subhuman status.

The spectacle of Baartman's body, however, continued even after her death at the age of twenty-six. Pseudo-scientists interested in investigating "primitive sexuality" dissected and cast her genitals in wax. Baartman, as far as we know, was the first person of Khosian-descent to be dismembered and displayed in this manner.

Anatomist Georges Curvier presented Baartman's dissected labia before the Academie Royale de Medecine, in order to allow them "to see the nature of the labia." Curvier and his contemporaries concluded that Baartman's oversized primitive genitalia was physical proof of African women's "primitive sexual appetite."

Baartman's genitalia continued to be exhibited at La Musée de l'Homme, the institution to which Curvier belonged, long after her death. This introduction to the history of human displays of people of color demonstrates that cultural difference and "otherness" were visually observed on the "Native" body," whether in live human exhibitions or dissected body parts on public display. Both forms of spectacle often served to promote Western colonial domination by configuring non-white cultures as being in need of discipline, civilization, and industry.

In post-apartheid South Africa, efforts were made to retrieve Saartjie's remains. In 1994, then-president Nelson Mandela appealed to his French counterpart, but it was not until 2002 that the French Senate approved a bill for repatriation of Saartjie's remains to South Africa. In May 2002, her remains were brought home to South Africa after nearly Two hundred years of humiliation and abuse. In August 2002, she was finally laid to rest in the Eastern Cape.

Sara Baartman's experience with exploitation was the beginning of a very dehumanizing existence for black women in white societies. Historically, the ability of black men to own property and develop means to lay down roots of security for his woman in America has been crippled by the socio-political landscape of post slavery America.

CHAPTER 3

Lighter Skin Tones Synonymous
with More Opportunities

From time to time, discussions arise among blacks concerning disparate treatment based on skin complexion, especially on the plantation during slavery. The terms "House-Servant" and "Field-Slave" eventually come up. In many regards, black women are still treated like modern-day field-slaves. Black women do not command the same respect as white women.

During slavery, in America, a "House-Servant" was typically a mulatto child fathered by the plantation's owner or white over-seer, who impregnated black women against their will. The disparate treatment between mulatto children, with lighter skin tones, and children with dark skin was reflected in mulatto children being assigned to easier chores around the house while children with dark skin performed backbreaking labor in the fields. Disparate treatment also meant mulatto children learned to read and write long before children with dark skin. These advantages often instilled a sense of privilege in children from mixed parents and secured preferences over slave children with black parents.

The outcome of disparate treatment produced a great psychological divide within the ranks of blacks in America. In general, the larger white community views blacks with lighter skin complexion as less likely to be violent, more trustworthy and more attractive.

Being made to feel less attractive, black women do not hesitate to attach a weave to their hair or wear wigs to make their hair look long and straight like that of white women. Black women are made to believe, by the preference of black men for white women, that their natural beauty is less desirable.

Because black women mask their natural hair and other natural African features, black men think, why should I go for the generic look when I can have the more-confident white woman? So, they choose white women. Unfortunately, black women live in a society that embraces the features of women of other races. Hollywood advertises their sexiest women, which may include Halle Berry whose father is black and mother is white. The traditional beautiful dark-skinned woman's natural beauty is not valued or embraced by American society. That is a tragedy because when you think of it, there is nothing more striking than a beautiful black woman. Angelina Jolie receives much attention with her lips that u are uncommonly thick. Thick lips are a common feature of black women.

The Census Bureau use to report on racial diversity in a very granular manner. It recorded exactly how many Negroes there were, how many mulattoes or biracial individuals, the number of whites with mixed parentage, the number of Indians with mixed blood, and the number of Hawaiians and part Malays there were. The boundaries between racial and ethnic groups, and even the definition of race and ethnicity, were blurred and contested. By 1930, however, this ambiguity largely disappeared from the census. Anyone with any "Negro blood" was counted as a Negro; whites no longer had mixed parentage; Indians were mainly identified by tribe rather than ancestry; and a consistent treatment of Asians was slowly developing across Asians immigrants from different Asian countries. Official government classification systems can create as well as reflect social, economic, and political inequality.

In his book, *"Disintegration, the Splintering of Black America,"* Eugene Robinson suggests that black America does not live here anymore. Eugene

Robinson does a wonderful job detailing the splintering of black America into four groups:

- A mainstream middle-class majority with full ownership stake in American society
- A large, abandoned minority with less hope of escaping poverty and dysfunction than at any time since Reconstruction's crushing end
- A small transcendent elite with enormous wealth, power, and influence.
- Two newly emergent groups-individuals of mixed-race heritage and communities of recent black immigrants-that makes us wonder what "black" is even supposed to mean.

This division in black America reflects social, economic, and political inequality against dark-skinned African Americans. Official classification defines groups, creates structurally the dominant group's belief about who belongs where, which groups deserve what, and ultimately who gets what. Private racial categories have affected whether an employer offers a person a job and whether a criminal defendant gets lynched.

Race is the pivot around which political contests about equality have been waged for most of this country's history. Since lighter-skin blacks have had more opportunities and made much more financial progress than black with darker skin tones, blacks with darker skin have pursued black women with lighter skin or women of other races and, in doing so avoided darker-skinned black women as if they symbolize little advancement from negative symbolism whites attach to dark-skinned blacks. The stigma of self-hatred is ingrained in the psyche of black men through their mistreatment and oppression as slaves. Black men, insecure of their black heritage, seek women of lighter skin tones or women of other races as a form of escape from a debased image. This behavior has been a consistent obsession of black men since the first black slave was integrated into white society.

Racial classification instruments have been used in America to generate inequality among races. Categorizations are unstable and impermanent. By studying the past century of racial classification in the United States, we can see how classification and inequality are related. From the Civil War era through the 1920s, the black population was partly deconstructed through official attention to mulattos then reconstructed through court decisions and state-level "one drop of blood" laws. This dropped the category of Mulatto in the Census data.

From the 1930s through the 1970s, the black population solidified though a growing sense of racial consciousness and shared fate. They also developed the political capacity to contest their poverty and unequal status. At this time, the transcendent group of black billionaires and Multi-Millionaires was not part of America's elite. Black solidarity proliferated in America not as a splintered black community, which Robinson suggested.

The category of mulatto disappeared, but the intra-group disparities that it implied did not. Inequalities among blacks, especially but not only in terms of skin color, have persisted into the twenty-first century with almost no public recognition.

The splintering of Black America is a case of the growth of a class structure and political disparity among blacks. A structure of inequality has emerged from a ranked social order created through a system of official racial classification. The US Census Bureau inventoried races by mixture, counting mulattos as a separate group from 1850 through 1920. It accepted the view that blacks and mulattos were meaningfully distinct. Census analysts meticulously documented differences in population growth rates, birth and death rates, school attendance and literacy, and migration patterns.

The report showed, for example, that "the proportion attending school in the population of school age among mulattoes exceeds the proportion among blacks in each section of the country." A few people saw mulattos as a separate race altogether. Social analyst Alfred Holt Stone argued in 1908 that:

- the mulatto is not a Negro, and
- there can no longer be a question as to the superior intelligence of the mulatto over the Negro

Such notions created inequalities in American society and stratified how blacks and mulattoes were treated. Among blacks and mulattoes, the inequalities covered all arenas-social, economic, and political. Well before the Civil War, the Census Bureau had noted the "preference they [mulattos] have enjoyed in the liberation from slavery" (Bureau of the Census 1864.)

Free mulattoes in the lower south were "afforded a status superior to that of Blacks," and they "tended to dominate the free black community in both numbers and influence. The lightest of the light-skinned lived almost as well as their White neighbors." Some owned slaves [(Jones 2000 1506-07-3). Among Union soldiers in the Civil War, lighter-skinned blacks held more skilled occupations and higher military ranks than their darker counterparts; they were taller (a measure of nutrition) and less likely to die in the war (Hochschild and Weaver 2007). Mulattos were more literate than blacks, and their children were more likely to attend school.

On average, mulattos also enjoyed economic advantages over blacks. Before the Civil War, free mulattos were more likely to own their own farms, and their households had much greater wealth than black households. Those differences continued, and perhaps deepened, after emancipation. "Complexion homogamy"—the tendency for people to marry others of a similar color-prevailed, and couples in which both spouses were mulatto had at least 30 to 90 percent more wealth than partnerships with at least one black.

Of the two black senators and twenty black members of Congress during Reconstruction, only three were not mulattos. Perhaps a majority of the prominent racial leaders of the era were light-skinned or had White ancestors, including Booker T. Washington, W. E. B. Du Bois, and A. Phillip Randolph. The status of mulattos was hardly risk-free, but in most cases they were better off than those with darker skin.

The danger of a splintered black America is that those who hold themselves up as the "better class" or part of a "privileged-group" on the caste of color does great harm to racial solidarity of black America. After emancipation, mulattoes erected a "color-caste" system within the race that is somewhat analogous to that prevailing in India. Black colleges and fraternities preferred light-skinned applicants; churches and organizations made distinctions in who could join or enter.

With the category of mulatto in existence, Jim Crow segregation could not be implemented. Under the one-drop rule, in which anyone with one drop of black blood was considered black, the whole concept of a group that was neither fully black nor white faded from social legitimacy.

The one-drop policy was associated with two immediate and related effects with regard to classification: the rejection of explicit multiracial identity within the group, and the suppression of recognition of skin color differences both within and outside the group. Neither blacks nor whites described mulattos any longer as evidence of a link between them, even if usually forced and shameful, or as a distinct category meaningful on its own terms.

Americans found it difficult to have a system of strict and elaborate segregation, such as Jim Crow, until they had eliminated the categories that blurred the lines between segregators and segregated. In societies that regard some races of people as dominant or superior and others as subordinate or inferior, hypo descent is the automatic assignment of children of a mixed union or mating between members of different socioeconomic groups or ethnic groups to the minority group. [1] The opposite practice is hyper descent, in which children are assigned to the race that is considered dominant or superior. The law of hypo descent and Jim Crow segregation generated or sustained several forms of inequality. Most obviously, black poverty and racial economic inequality persisted and perhaps worsened.

Black America splintering into four groups ushers in the beginning of very dark times for black America. Intra-racial hostility and mistrust of the different goals of splintered black America prevents the group from consolidating into a powerful movement to contest structures of economic and political inequality. The problem confronting black America is a microcosm of why the poor in the United States have not wrested political control from the few rich. Black America and middle-class white America are deeply divided by racial animosity and mistrust.

In the 1961 survey of southern blacks, family income and years of education were both higher for those identified as light-skinned, and declined proportionally with darker pigments. The 1968 Kerner Commission survey, of blacks in fifteen major American cities, yielded the same results. This pattern of light-skin advantage within the black population has persisted to the present, and ranges across arenas as diverse as the likelihood of marrying, visual representation in the media, the length of prison sentences, the chances of becoming a political candidate and winning elective office, and the selection to a judgeship (Hochschild and Weaver 2007).

Skin tone is a much more fraught topic, and much less part of the public discourse, than is multiracialism. Nevertheless, differential treatment by skin color is arguably more implicated in racial inequality and racially-inflected poverty than is multiracial heritage. People of mixed race on average have a socioeconomic status (SES) between the averages of their parents' racial group. Socioeconomic status is commonly conceptualized as the social standing or class of an individual or group. It is often measured as a combination of education, income and occupation. Examinations of socioeconomic status often reveal inequities in access to resources, plus issues related to privilege, power and control multiracial identifiers on the 2000 Census were somewhat younger, better educated, and more urban than mono-racial identifiers (Hochschild 2005). So multi-racials are relatively well-off compared with the average black.

Not so for dark-skinned African Americans. Many scholars, using the eight national surveys with a skin color measure as well as local or more opportunistic surveys, have reached the same conclusion: darker skin color within a given race or ethnicity is associated with lower SES. The 2107 respondents of the 1979-1980 National Survey of Black Americans (NSBA;) (Jackson and Gurin 1987), for example, averaged 10.9 years of schooling. But a gap of almost two years separated the schooling of the darkest and lightest among those surveyed. The pattern is the same for income: blacks' mean family income in NSBA was $12,417, with almost a $5000 annual difference in family income between the lightest—and darkest-skinned respondents. Put another way, dark-skinned blacks earned less than 70 percent as much as light-skinned blacks, during a year in which black families' mean income was 63 percent of that of white families. People of all races treat light-skinned blacks differently from dark-skinned blacks.

Tiger Woods and Michael Jackson are very well loved and adored by millions worldwide. Their lives exemplify the mindset of the twenty-first century black man in America. They downplayed the significance of their African heritage by seeking refuge from black roots. In order for other races to embrace them, celebrities find it financially paramount to integrate into the larger white society, leaving black women to defend her honor alone.

Although Tiger Wood's mother has Asian ancestry and his father is of African descent, Tiger did not hesitate to marry a Swedish woman with blond hair and blue eyes. Did Tiger, at any time, ever consider marrying a black woman? Black men can fool some of the people all the time but the truth ultimately will come to light. At the end of the day, as Michael Jackson stated, you "must look at the man in the mirror." By the end of his life, Michael Jackson, a black man, preferred being a father to kids who could pass as white. It is mind boggling the changes that money can create in a lifetime. The moral lesson from Michael Jackson's life story is "if you do not love and embrace yourself, all the women of other races and money in the world will not make you happy."

Bi-racial children, from black/white unions, have a choice of adopting black or white ethnicity. The selection of women of other races by bi-racial men tells you a lot about their worldview. Tiger Woods chose a white woman; President Obama, although mixed-race, chose a strong black woman. President Obama's choice suggests that he is more in touch with his African ancestry. To her credit, Halle Berry tried to select a black man, but they were abusive. Like other abused black women, Halle ended up selecting a white man to father her child.

By his choice of women, Tiger Wood is more heavily influence d by his mother's ancestry by referring to himself as "Cablinasian." Michael Jackson not only chose white women to marry; he purposely chose to be a father to children's who appears to be white. What was it about Michael Jackson that caused him to alter natural African features such as his nose and hair to assume the physical characteristics of a white person? It has been reported that Michael Jackson saw his natural African features as ugly. Not embracing his natural African features proved to be Michael Jackson's greatest tragedy. Imagine the insecurity in such a talented individual.

For Tiger, Michael, and a starstruck society, image is everything. Both of these men embraced white culture and each believed profoundly in using women of other races in their efforts to distance themselves from a stereotype of black inferiority.

The image of happy and successful black couples, like Ossie Davis and Ruby Dee, or Michelle and Barack Obama is becoming rare. Although President Obama is biracial, no one can ever mistake him as a white person. Whites have no problem when wealthy black men choose to rescue white women and empower them rather than help black women. When celebrity status, wealth, and power are represented in a black man, white men tolerate black men with white women. It is easier for white men to embrace wealthy black men approach to white women because, when there is a misstep, white women will get considerable compensation for her involvement.

It is no secret that black women are less adored in society than Caucasian or black women with lighter skin. Blacks with lighter skin pigmentation continue to have better opportunities than blacks with darker skin tones.

Prior to the 1960's in black communities, among the black elite there was a disproportionate number of blacks with light-skin tones, and to gain access to better black social circles, it helped blacks to be able to pass the "paper bag test." Blacks who had what was referred to as "good hair" and "fair-skin" were well respected. "Good hair" was straight and not kinky, curly, or what was referred to as "kuckabulbs." Light-skinned boyfriends or girlfriends were considered prizes in black communities because white features were considered more attractive than African features.

To this very day, black women, with dark-skin and their dark-skinned babies, have not transcended negative racial stereotyping. They remain less influential than white men, white women and black men.

There is still subtle conflict and jealousy between women of dark complexion and black and white women with lighter skin tones. Producer and Director, Spike Lee illustrated the conflict between black women of different complexions in his movie "*School Daze.*" Black men's pursuit of white women adds uncertainty to the psyche of black women. This dilemma is a significant threat to the survival of the black community.

Many black women would agree that black men are carrying dating women of other races way too far. Forty-two percent of black women have never been married (ABC Nightline, Linsey Davis and Hana Karar, Dec 22, 2009). For many black men, the desire for social approval, especially from whites, increases with the degree of their economic, occupational, and material success. Thus, the desire to be "treated" and "perceived" as "equal" tends to intensify as the black man attempts to validate himself by "copying" the white man in all other spheres of life. Yet, the stain of inferiority and inequality remains stamped upon his unconscious.

Interracial dating is a luxury black people, as a whole, cannot afford. The splintering of black America into the four groups transcendent, middle class, abandoned, and the emergent mixed class has divided the black community and ushered in a self mentality that is very dangerous to blacks in a world where black people are not respected. For some reason, black men seem to have a target on their backs, and we, as black people must never forget the past. I think black people would be wise to guard their existence and unite, much in the manner of the Jews after the Holocaust.

It seems that the economically transcendent blacks find it all too easy to forget the trials and tribulations of slavery. Blacks would be wise to learn from Jewish people how to guard against the second coming of a holocaust. Until every black man and woman prospers, black men's abandonment of a large segment of middle-class black women is a formula for disaster for blacks. Black men are demonstrating that they are vulnerable prey for women of other races. While reveling in sex with women of other race, black men are not keeping their eyes on what Martin Luther King Jr. referred to as the "*Prize.*" For the most part the "*Prize*" starts and ends with black women.

Historically, I can understand disrespect, from a competitive perspective, by members of other races, both male and female, for black women. It all comes down to survival of the fittest. Competition for power and control between races dates back to ancient Rome, Greece, China, and oldest civilizations in Ethiopia. There is currently a very disturbing trend whereby black men not supporting black women. What's very disheartening is the open complicity of black men to secure the lives of women of other races, while black women struggle to survive in a very hostile economic market place. When black men turn their backs on black women, they are consciously obscuring black roots to secure an illusion of acceptance into the larger society that maintains a timeless apprehensive, if not fear-based insecurity, when dealing with black people, especially blacks with really dark skin.

It is disturbing observing successful black men deserting their ethnicity to sniff the butts of women of other races, who would not give them the time of day if black men had no money. How do black men explain this bazaar behavior to the little black boys and girls who are growing up and witnessing this disregard for their black mothers? Black men's disrespect of black women as potential mothers to his children shows disrespect of his own mother. A man who cannot respect his own origin has serious issues.

CHAPTER 4

Inside the Rage of Black Women

During slavery, black women had little rights, legal recourse, or protection from local, state or federal authorities. Black were considered less than human and bred like animals, and sold off like an animal. A black woman had little or no control over decisions concerning her life. There were no battered women's shelters, NOW movements, rape crisis centers, NAACP, civil rights advocates, or any other support system sympathetic to the injustice and unhappiness black women suffered. She was completely incapable of rejecting her white slave master's wishes. She had two choices: to do or die.

Rape is not an aggressive expression of sexuality, but a sexual expression of aggression. In the perpetrator's psyche, it does not fulfill sexual functions, but is a manifestation of anger, violence and domination. The purpose is to degrade, humiliate and subjugate that person. Forcible entry into the body is the severest attack imaginable on the most intimate self and dignity of a person.

In general, it is a characteristic of severe torture. Entering a woman's body by force has effects that are comparable to torture: it causes physical pain, the loss of personal dignity and self-determination, and is an attack on the woman's identity.

Any struggle for dignity and self-determination is rooted in the control of one's own body, primarily the control of physical access to one's body. In most case, a rape victim does not feel she is exposed to a sexual act but to an extreme and humiliating form of violence directed against herself and her body. Even rapists themselves hardly ever speak of a sexual experience. Instead, they express feelings of hostility, aggression, power, and dominance.

Rapists also tend to depersonalize their victims. They hardly perceive the woman as an individual and, if they did not know her before, are often unable to describe her afterwards. For the rapist, the victim is "women as such" and not a concrete person. This explains why rapists seldom have pity on their victims or feel guilty toward them. In sum, we can say in the act of rape, the perpetrator's sexuality is not an end in itself. Rather, it is used as an instrument to exert violence.

White men's treatment of black women was the beginning of the soiling of black women in America. It must have been devastating for male slaves to witness the disrespect of black women. There has been some healing from the trauma of these acts, but the archetypical scarring remains with black people as the Holocaust of World War II remains with Jewish people. Harsh treatment of black women during slavery established a negative image that has been difficult for black women to shed.

Black women were reduced to being ejaculatory dumping grounds to increase the slave population, which helped create enormous wealth for white people. There is no denying that white men have had a chief hand in undermining the self-esteem of black women. This is the primary reason black women are less likely than black males or white women to enter interracial relationships. Some black males enter into interracial relationships motivated by vengeance; others enter them to overcome inferiority complexes; others out of curiosity.

The history of black women as slaves reveals they were devalued and relegated to a laboring slut. Every inch of the black woman was used for toil without compensation: her head to carry heavy loads; her breasts to feed white children; her hands to pick cotton, wash clothes, and till the soil; her legs as transport through this torture; and her vagina, anus, and breasts to pacify and please her persecutors.

Other Forms of Reckless Regard for Women of Color

The rapid changes occurring in society with the development of a new "educated" elite have resulted in a change of attitude on the part of people in various positions of power: even those with very limited power. One example is the effort to control black population growth through a form of carefully concealed violence perpetrated on helpless medical patients.

Dorothy Roberts reports in *Killing the Black Body: Race, Reproduction, and the Meaning of Liberty* that during the 1970s, sterilization became the most rapidly growing form of birth control in the United States, rising from two hundred thousand cases in 1970 to over seven hundred thousand in 1980. "It was a common belief among blacks in the South," Roberts writes,

> **B**lack women were routinely sterilized without their informed consent and for no valid medical reason. Teaching hospitals performed unnecessary hysterectomies on poor black women as practice for their medical residents. This sort of abuse was so widespread in the South that these operations came to be known as "Mississippi appendectomies."

> In 1975, a hysterectomy cost $800 compared to a tubal ligation, giving surgeons, who were reimbursed by Medicaid, a financial incentive to perform the more extensive operation despite its 20 times greater risk of killing the patient.

> Fannie Lou Hamer, the leader of the Mississippi Freedom Democratic Party, informed a Washington, D.C., audience in 1965 that 60 percent of the black women in Sunflower County, Mississippi, were subjected to postpartum sterilizations at Sunflower City Hospital without their permission. Hamer had suffered this violation herself

when she went to the hospital for the removal of a small uterine tumor in 1961. The doctor took the liberty of performing a complete hysterectomy without her knowledge or consent. This practice of sterilizing Southern Black women through trickery or deceit was confirmed by a number of physicians who examined these women after the procedure was performed.

"Sterilization abuse was not confined to hospitals in the South," Roberts continues

In April 1972, the Boston Globe ran a front-page story reporting the complaint by a group of medical students that Boston City Hospital was performing excessive and medically unnecessary hysterectomies on black patients. Among the charges were: surgeries were performed for "training purposes"; radical and dangerous procedures were used when alternatives were available; medical records did not reflect what had really been done to patients; patients were pressured into signing consent forms without adequate explanation; and doctors treated patients callously, adding to the women's anguish."

The attitude behind these illegal sterilizations is very similar to the distorted attitudes toward black females in general, regardless of their age, one hundred fifty years ago. For example:

. . . when George, a Mississippi slave, was convicted and sentenced to death in 1859 for the rape of a ten-year-old female slave, Judge Harris reversed the decision and released George. According to Harris the original indictment could not be sustained under common law or under the statutes of Mississippi because "it charges no offense known to either system . . . There is no act that embraces either the attempted or actual commission of a rape by a slave on a female slave." (Tribe.net, June 8, 2007, Black Women Were Sterilized Until the 1970 in the United States)

A Tennessee judge made this latter point when he remanded a slave named Grandison to jail for attempting to rape a white woman named Mary Douglas. According to Judge Green, what gave "the offense its enormity" was the fact that Douglas was white. "Such an act committed on a BLACK WOMAN, would not,' he noted, "be punished with death" (Deborah Gray White, *Ar'n't I a Woman? Female Slaves in Plantation South).*

Since recorded history, women of all ethnic groups have been made victims because of their sex. This is true, despite the fact some women are physically stronger than men, have more endurance than men, and are capable of doing manual labor even better than men.

Such a woman was the slave Susan Mabry of Virginia, who could pick four hundred or five hundred pounds of cotton a day. However, one hundred fifty to two hundred pounds were considered respectable for an average worker.

In *Labor of Love, Labor of Sorrow* (1986), Jacqueline Jones writes:

> "Together with their fathers, husbands, brothers, and sons, black women spent up to fourteen hours a day toiling out of doors, often under a blazing sun. In the Cotton Belt they plowed fields; dropped seed; and hoed, picked, ginned, sorted, and moted cotton. On farms in Virginia, North Carolina, Kentucky, and Tennessee, women hoed tobacco; laid worm fences; and threshed, raked, and bound wheat.

> "For those on the Sea Islands and in coastal areas, rice culture included raking and burning the stubble from the previous year's crop; ditching; sowing seed; plowing, listing, and hoeing fields; and harvesting, stacking, and threshing the rice. In the bayou region of Louisiana, women planted sugar cane cuttings, plowed, and helped to harvest and gin the cane.

"During the winter, they performed a myriad of tasks necessary on nineteenth century farms . . . During the busy harvest season, everyone was forced to labor up to sixteen hours at a time after sunset by the light of candles or burning pine knots . . . It is significant that overseers ordered and supervised much of the punishment in the field, for their disciplinary techniques were calculated to get as much work out of the slaves as they can possibly perform.

"Consequently, many slave women were driven and beaten mercilessly, and some achieved respite only in return for sexual submission. To white men, black women were not only workers who needed prodding, but also females capable of fulfilling his sexual or aggressive desires. For this reason, a fine line existed between work-related punishment and rape."

The mold was already formed when slavery "officially" ended.

For many years, it was nearly impossible for black women to assume roles other than those they had held in slavery. Many white Americans, even today, continue to perceive African American women as individuals who can be worked hard, treated rudely, and who desire promiscuous relationships.

From the official end of slavery in 1865, with the Thirteenth Amendment to the Constitution, through almost all of the twentieth century, no Southern white male was convicted of raping or attempting to rape a black woman. And if the perpetrator were black, the black woman still had no hope for justice. When a black man raped a black woman, police nearly always reported the crime as "unfounded," and in the few cases that reached the courts, the testimony of black female victims was seldom believed by white juries.

Unbelievable as it may seem, one of the reasons given as proof that black women in the United States are naturally promiscuous is the fact that prior to the American Revolution the female slave population grew more as a result of natural increase than by importation. Unlike other

Western Hemisphere countries with slavery, the United States achieved a one-to-one sex ratio the same number of women as men, although far more men were brought from Africa.

One reason for this was the creation of monogamous families in this country, while in Latin America and the Caribbean, black men were forced to live in barrack-like environments away from the women.

However, this fact did not make the US slaves as well off as it may appear. North American male slaves were more easily manipulated, since their spouses and children could be held hostage and compelled to answer for their husbands and fathers' "transgressions." During the nineteenth century, when "protecting women" was almost a part of the national religion, only slave women were so totally unprotected by men or the law. Only African American women had their womanhood so totally denied.

Yet, in spite of the great gulf between white and black women at the time, their lives were paradoxically similar. All women were overwhelmed by work. Slave and free women alike had no visible control over reproduction. Both were forced to relinquish control over this highly personal aspect of female life to white males, who made all crucial decisions regarding the future of the children.

They even decided whether there would be an abortion. Have the times changed very much today? "Relative to white men all women were powerless and exploited," says Deborah Gray White. (Tribe.net, Black Women Were Sterilized Until 1970 in the United States, June 8, 2007)

> The powerlessness and exploitation of black women was an extreme form of what all women experienced, because racism, although just as pervasive as sexism, was more virulent. Slave women suffered from the malevolence that flowed from both racism and sexism.

> Of all large groups of people in the United States today, black women are treated the worst, any way you look at it. There's less respect for them, fewer jobs, less of everything that is needed for an even half-way decent life.

An increasing proportion of them, as well as black men, will exist outside the world of gainful employment as long as the capitalist system prevails in this country.

It is our task today to see to it that this system is replaced by a new society run by and for working people and their allies through socialism. History is supposed to give people a sense of identity, a knowledge of who they are and why they are living as they are. It should also act as a springboard for the future. History must replace myths with facts. We Americans of all colors, especially African American women, have had enough myths. Despite all that she has lived through and accomplished, the black woman today is still waiting for an affirmative answer to the plaintive question asked one hundred fifty years ago: "Ar'n't I a woman?"

Professor Michael Eric Dyson stated succinctly in his book *Why I Love Black Women,*

"Spurning black women cannot be considered an exclusively personal or private choice of black men in an erotic and emotional vacuum . . . it must be seen as part of a deeply rooted, if often unconscious, process of pursuing the emblem of beauty and status from which black men have been historically barred."

Alienation, abandonment, and struggle are some things many black women know very well. Living without a loving male companion can be frightening as well as challenging for black women. It is a tough world, much like a jungle, with pitfalls all along the way. More and more, black men, once educated and successful, are bankrolling women of other races and showing great insensitivity to the challenges of black women.

Without the strength, courage, and support of smart and educated black men, many black women, very strong and resilient, struggle to find balance and happiness with the love of a strong black men in their lives. Black women are disregarded and misunderstood by men and women of other ethnicities. On top of that, black women are continually confronted with a promiscuous mentality in black men. Black men are supposed to be black women's loyal protector. Sadly, black women are left behind by successful black men who seek women of other races as mates.

According to a 2005 study done at Columbia University by Aaron Gullickson, blacks with college degrees are 35 percent more likely to enter into interracial marriages than blacks with less education, and lower-class blacks showed, "strong isolation from the interracial marriage market." Whites who marry blacks engage in cherry-picking, removing only the most successful individuals from a disadvantaged minority community sorely in need of successful role models. The Columbia study showed no correlation between educational level and interracial marriage for white spouses of blacks. Black men will use any excuse necessary to gain access to the forbidden fruits of women of other races.

It is sad that black men choose to desert black women. The desecration of black women's image as promiscuous and confrontational is a continuation of the cultural rape and kiss of death to black women. The disrespect of black women happens so frequently that at times political correctness is abandoned, because there are those who feel as if open season on attacking racial minorities should be the rule rather than the exception.

On April 4, 2007, during a discussion about the NCAA Women's Basketball Championship, radio and television personality Don Imus characterized the Rutgers University women's basketball team players (dark-skinned black women) as "rough girls," when commenting on their tattoos. Don Imus's executive producer, Bernard McGuirk, responded by referring to them as "hardcore hos [whores]." The discussion continued, with Imus describing the girls as "nappy-headed hos" and McGuirk remarking that the two teams looked like the "jigaboos versus the wannabes" mentioned in Spike Lee's film, School Daze, apparently referring to the two team's differing appearances.

At 6:00 P.M. Media Matters for America released recorded transcripts to the news media highlighting the brief exchange:

Imus: That's some rough girls from Rutgers. Man, they
got tattoos and—

McGuirk: Some hard-core hos (whores).

Imus: That's some nappy-headed hos. I'm gonna tell you
that now, man, that's some—whew. And the girls
from Tennessee, they all look cute; you know, so,
like—kind of like—I don't know.

McGuirk: A Spike Lee thing.

Imus: Yeah.

McGuirk: The Jigaboos vs. the Wannabes.

White males are obsessed with the success of their future offspring
and have guarded their women jealously. Black men should take notice
of this attribute in white men. White men are reluctant to choose a black
female as a life mate, as that choice may influence the success of their
future children.

To further illustrate white male consideration of black females, in
his interview with *Playboy*, John Mayer, a world-famous musician, who
performed at Michael Jackson's memorial, was asked if black women threw
themselves at him, Mayer responded, "I don't think I open myself to it
[dating black women]. My dick is sort of like a White Supremacist. I've
got a Benetton heart and a fucking David Duke cock." David Duke is a
Ku Klux Klan member from Louisiana. John Mayer's statement translates
into his white dick being too good for black women. Many white men
hold that view.

Plain and simple, this is how black women are viewed and regarded.
What does this really say about black men who voluntarily participate in
the destruction of his women and race?

Black men stigmatize their own women as bitchy, confrontational,
and violent to justify choosing women of other races. In reality, the
white woman is the black man's way of crossing over into the white
mainstream.

Michael Jackson, Koby Bryant, Charles Barkley, and Tiger Woods,
and other celebrity "black superstars," are shining examples of wealthy

black men who have allowed the comfort of wealth to eliminate black women as matrimonial prospects. Lusting after white women and fulfilling sexual cravings with an interracial flavor continues to reveal disquieting traitorous attributes in black men. It is easy to see how Africa was so easily infiltrated and destroyed by other races. Black men are less loyal and less vigilant to the needs of their women.

Black men's fascination with women of other races is an attempt to overcome an inferiority image. By dating women of other races, a black man seeks to demonstrate that he has transcended that inferior image. Unfortunately for black women, if black men succeed in shedding this self-image of inferiority, it comes at the price of demonstrating loyalty to women of other races. In doing so, many prosperous black men hope to change the complexity and degree of his struggle for viability in the larger society by abandoning decaying black neighborhoods.

The first strike against black women is their fidelity to black culture and ethnicity. To many prosperous black men, fidelity to ethnicity can be a financial kiss of death. In the work place, black people are expected to groom their hair in a manner that is not offensive to whites, walk and talk in a certain manner, and dress a certain way. The more black people conform to white values, the more likely they are to be rewarded. It is very difficult for black men to be truly happy with a caricature-like, deceptive, outward appearance of what whites expect of him and their disregard for who he truly is as a black man.

When seeking the love of women of other races for purposes of inclusiveness in the larger society, black men present a deceptive outward appearance. This is evident in the case of O.J. Simpson, a well-regarded, successful, black professional athlete who many black women feel sold out by marrying a white woman. His first wife was black, but he could not stay faithful in his marriage with access to so many other women, including those of other races.

In the end, the deceptive outward appearance of a made-over black man caved in to a dormant psychosis created by an inferiority complex. Tiger Wood's infidelity troubles may be symptomatic of the identity crisis most black men suffer, as they seek inclusiveness with wealth and attempt to overcome the negative stigma associated with being black in a white man's world. The very thing black women love the most is the black man. For black men to submit capriciously what black women love the most to women of other races is, in many ways, the rape of her spirit.

The second strike against black women is her strength and how she challenges black men to embrace his ethnicity and history. She also challenges him not to succumb to ideas of inferiority and shame planted in his psyche by the larger society because of his dark skin.

In today's society, it is difficult for the black man to celebrate his black ancestry. As it stands for black American men, his roots lead him back to slavery. He will not be rewarded in corporate America if he looks black, shares his contrary political thoughts, or even entertains the thought that Jesus may have been a black man. A black woman could have saved Michael Jackson from his pain and torture by making him feel that his black-skin and African features were okay. She can also save other black men who are struggling to ignore their blackness in a white man's world.

Despite all the things a black woman can provide for a black man, she cannot provide the illusion that he has transcended the negative racial stereotype of his African heritage. Black women are about preserving black families. The black woman is the only way the black race will survive; deny her children freedom, life, and happiness, and the destruction of black civilization remains a possibility.

By gender and class, black women are at the bottom of the social ladder and need the assistance of financially viable black men. With black men growing ability to wed women of other races, black women are being forced to turn to white men. Most black women choose not to go the interracial route, preferring to hold out for a good black man.

The timing for black men's turning away from black women could not be worse, considering the volatile economic conditions of today. It would be a different matter if black America were not divided as it is currently. It just seems to me that instead of stepping up his game and uplifting black women, black men obsessed with short-term gratification are all too willing to throw out the baby with the wash by abandoning black women.

We live in a society where drugs and alcohol play a large role in hyping sexual pleasure. There is so much pressure to hold a job that addiction to sedatives is a very serious problem in many relationships. Stress influences including alcohol and drugs in lifestyles to sedate the stress in time consuming, and demanding high tech industries. Many decisions to commit infidelity and exhibit abusive behaviors are encouraged by drugs and alcohol.

Public scandal suggests celebrities are not satisfied isolated inside their "ivory towers" with their white trophy wives. They married women of other races, because black women are not the ticket for cross-over acceptance once inside the privileged arena. It is apparent that many affluent black men are uncomfortable in lily-white environments with a black woman.

Once black men achieve prosperity and move out of black environments, they are surrounded by white men who care more about money than chasing women. With money, white men know that women can be had for a price. Black men, in these circles, tend to go overboard, as Tiger Woods did when he pursued as many white women as possible. Is this what black men truly desire once they are financially stable? If given a choice, do all black men want to chase white women?

I arrived in California in April of 1974. I was fresh out of the Georgia woods. I would be lying if I said I was not fascinated by white women. I was interested, because in segregated Georgia, because white men went through so much trouble to keep black men away from white women. I always wondered what the difference was in the skin texture, the texture of the hair, the color of the eyes, and why blond hair was lighter in the summer and darker in the winter. Of course, white guys in the South were constantly talking about oral sex with white girls, so I was more than curious how these little white prima donnas went from angels to devils in the bedroom.

So, with no barrier between them and me in California, I experimented. I have to say I was thrilled because I encountered little resistance in having

41

sex anyway I wanted with them. Once the curiosity was satisfied, there were no special qualities that made white women any more desirable to me than black women.

I think all black men are somewhat curious about women of other races until they have experienced intimacy with them. It has been my experience that black women's skin texture and tone, and breasts and buttocks are in a class of their own. The eye color and long hair of women of other races have their attractiveness. Beautiful women abound in each race. I think black men were more impressed with the wealth and education of women of other races. Only black men who are experiencing some degree of self-hatred choose to date women of other races "exclusively," because black women are educated today, many are financially secure, and black beauty is certainly in a league of its own.

NFL running back Tiki Barber, heavyweight boxing champ Jack Johnson (whom had three white wives), and Barack Obama Sr. illustrates black men who married women of other races and ended up disrespecting them. If they truly loved their wives, they would respect them. So, by virtue of the levels of disrespect shown to their women and the inability to honor them truly with love, was there ever love? Why did they really marry women of other races? Why are the women with whom these men have extra-marital affairs white? Each of these men went from one white woman to another. What factors guided them away from the arms of black women?

Women of other races manipulate black men's fantasy cravings and certainly benefit financially. Things may have worked out differently for O.J. Simpson, Michael Jackson, Charles Barkley, and Tiger Woods if they had chosen a strong, black woman committed to preserving a positive black image for black people. Barack Obama's, Will Smith's, and Denzel Washington's marriages may have their challenges, but they are inspiring examples of black men committed to loving black women.

From the ongoing escapades and infidelities of successful athletes, businessmen and even many average black guys in the neighborhood, it is clear that it is not black women who have the major issues. Not only are many black men proving unworthy of the love of black women, they are proving they are not worthy of women of other races either. The sad part is the majority of black men are in denial of their use of women of other races as image enhancers. Even though a black woman can be more stunning, she does not contribute to the ego of black men who value an image of access to the forbidden sexual fruits from women of other races.

People often leave a of trail of pain or of happiness much like a jet leaves vapor trails of burning fuel in the sky. Pain and pleasure are the trace elements in the vapor trails in the lives of black women who have dealt with promiscuous black men exclusively fixated on women of other races. These men seem to be void of a sensitivity that would promote respect for themselves and their women.

The vapor trails of black women's struggles include their dismal relationships with spouses (black males) and their struggle with opportunistic women of other races who are intimidated by black women's beauty, strength, and intelligence.

Black women certainly continue to struggle with lower wages, on average than Asian or white women. The black-white gap in job losses is greater among women. Specifically, black women have lost 5.2 percent of their jobs in the year ending October 2009, while white women lost 2.5 percent. That's a ratio of 2.1:1. (Family In equality, Phillip Cohen, Nov, 14, 2009)

Employment Gains and Wage Declines: The Erosion of Black Women's Relative Wages Since 1980," authors Becky Pettit and Stephanie Ewert, write "In the late 1970s, white women's wages were less than 5% more than black women's, and they are now more than 10% higher, closer to 15% higher for young workers."

These groups—black men, women of other races, and white men—are the three obstacles encountered in the course of a black woman's life, as she attempts to gain the respect and find her niche in society.

Kobe and Tiger could have married black women. White families are hard-pressed to accept the interracial union if the black man has no financial resources. Wealthy black athletes very rarely marry white women from well-established families.

Approximately 98 percent of the white women married to black men have gained within the arrangement a financial quality of life benefit these black men tend to ignore. Take a quick look at the all-to-prevalent NBA and NFL interracial marriages and you will find dark-skinned, nappy-headed men married to blond haired, Anglo-Saxon, model-type beauties. Would this have even been possible had these men not been millionaires? How many instances can we point to in which white women marry down in socioeconomic status? If love is blind, why is it so difficult to find a rich white woman married to a poor black man? Interracial relationships between black men and non-African women are about self-hatred, rejection of black women, and financial exploitation by non-African women who are able to become wealthy at the expense of the black man's self-hatred. There are exceptions to every rule but the obvious cannot be denied. This is a slap in the face, by black men, to deserving black women.

Denzel Washington has made many overtures to remaining faithful to an image that celebrates black women. I admire his stance in tempering his sexual involvement with white women in his personal life and in movies. Through their actions, Denzel Washington and President Barrack Obama demonstrate how black men should nurture the spirit of black women and are very aware of the message they send to young black men that instructs them to value and participate in the renaissance of respect for black women.

It is disappointing that the list is growing of black men who have no remorse for their acts and readily concede their ethnicity for a sexual romp with women of other races. Overwhelmed by a potent sex drive, black men are focused on their selfish sex drives and oblivious to the fundamental needs of black women, which includes fidelity in relationships.

Black men must honestly question what, in their value system, leads them to prefer white women over black women. Is it the sex; is it Hollywood, or is it too much of a problem for black men to be "black"? When did black men become so secure in American society that they could afford not to keep their eye on the prize as Martin Luther King Jr. urged?

Black men in America, supposedly symbols of strength for black women, are increasingly sources of disappointment to black women. Why do black men with wealth become so enigmatic about their commitment to black women? Back in the day, on the plantation, not only were black men infuriated with white men for raping and beating black women, but they were also resentful of the "preferential treatment" given to bi-racial men and women produced from rape and abuse of black women by white slave owners and overseers. The white slave owner's seeds were given preferential treatment over non-biracial slaves.

If we fast-forward the actors from slavery to modern times, as soon as black men attained freedom, they flipped the script and subjected black women to a different kind of abuse by turning away from them and worshipping women of other races. In essence, they turned to the very same women who were partners in crime in the assault on black women. Black men leave their women behind, seeking refuge from their black genealogy and an ethnicity painfully rich with a history of crime, sorrow, and economic hardship. Black women and their babies are left to struggle alone in society.

In the movie *Precious,* the greatest damage was done by an absent black man who lacked the capacity to honor his wife. Not only did he abuse his woman, but the sickness of an insatiable need for sex also drove him to rape his daughter and impregnate her twice. The movie focused on the relationship between the mother and the daughter. To me, the most appalling aspect of the plot was the damage done by a black man to both women. Whether black men are absent because the attraction of women of other races, locked up for falling into the trap of a life of crime, or absent simply because they just do not have it in themselves to man up to the responsibilities brought on through reckless sexual escapades, the bottom line is that black men are becoming irresponsibly unavailable to black women.

CHAPTER 5

Animosity and Jealousy Between Black and White Women

From my experiences, White women are very happy and comfortable in the presence of a confident and self-assured black man. If anything, her black lover's willingness to be with her in the presence of other black women and white men makes him even more intriguing to her.

When interracial couples come together, physical differences are very obvious. The different colors of the eyes, the texture and length of hair, the contrasting tan lines of white women in the summer and the smell of their breath and hair are all strikingly different from those of black women.

There is something else that comes about when a black man and a white woman get together. It seem the white woman offers a quiet refuge, where the black man can relax. Somehow, the haven provided by a white woman is similar to what one would feel if one were in trouble in a foreign country and sought refuge at an embassy. Black men actually feel like they are breaking a rule. It is empowering to control sensual situations and women who, at one point in history, just looking at her could have caused him to be hanged. Black men seek these opportunities with an unmatched fervor.

Exploring the differences in racial attributes behind closed doors is the captivating allure of forbidden fruit. It is the same curiosity that caused Eve to eat from the Tree of Knowledge. Gaining the acceptance and confidence of women of other races is an affirmation of inclusion that has become paramount for many black men. Gaining the trust and affection of women of other races becomes a symbol of triumph through defiance.

One can wonder if white women, once partner in crimes with white males against black men and women, now, submit themselves to black men in sacrificial sexual rituals to cleanse their guilty conscience and help heal the anger in black men, but in doing so, they further the pain of black women by diminishing the number of black men available in the black women's dating pool.

White men have gone to extreme measures, which include castration, public whippings, hangings, decapitations, drowning, and other despicable behaviors to curtail black men's interactions with white women. Yet, white men violated black women at will. With all the extreme measures white men have taken to protect and shelter white women, black men become more motivated and curious to have what has been traditionally denied to him; sexual freedom with women of other colors.

When it comes to black men and interracial dating, black women find his eagerness to the racial divide very unsettling. Research indicates that the number of black men dating or marrying outside of their race is much greater than that of black women. Black men going the interracial route is much like mice jumping off a sinking ship; black women "do" get it! They are being abandoned.

Black women are not so much concerned that other women are taking black men. It is disturbing to them that black men use multiple generations of struggle and suffering of oppressed forefathers and foremothers to glorify not black daughters but women of other races. This evil, perpetrated by black men on black women, is greater than anything other people have ever done.

Women of other races are conditioned to believe they have superior status to black women. It is understood that black women must be twice as good to be considered half as good as her white female counterpart. In vigilantly maintaining heir perceived entitlements, many white women have not united with their black sister to stem racial transgressions suffered by women of color. The phrase "Behind every great man there is a great woman, implies that when evil men finished their days work, they had to come home to share the spoils of their evil.

White women could have persuaded their husbands to be kinder and compassionate towards other races. I would think that greed could push morality into the back ground. Through the voting process, a large percentage of white women are compliant with the harsh treatment by white males towards people of color. Naturally, her compliance, with the will of white men, has created undercurrents of uneasiness in her relations with black women. If the two women were united, they could move mountains.

Animosity and jealousy between black women and white women have roots that run deep into the womb of slavery. The social status of white women was determined by white people's relationship with themselves, men and women, and black people. It was the enslavement of African people in colonized America that marked a big change in social status for white women.

Prior to slavery, white women were little more than glorified laborers with their lives spent in a master-servant relationship with white men. The enslavement of black people allowed white women to vacate their lowly position and assume an upgraded status.

White men institutionalized slavery, but white women were its immediate beneficiaries. White women differentiated their status by treating slaves in a brutal and cruel manner. It was with the black female slave that white women asserted most of their power; and black women resented the power of white females.

Even as a slave, black women expressed contempt and disregard for white female authority. As a result, the white mistress resorted to brutal punishment to reinforce her power over black females. Brutal punishment only increased resentment of black women for white women. There is a noticeable undercurrent of this contention between black and white women to this very day.

Having access and total control over the bodies of black women, white men's sexual exploitation of black women created even more tension between white women and black women. White women did not envy black women's role as a sexual object; they only feared her newly acquired social status was being threatened by her mate's sexual lust for the mysterious, exotic, and luscious black female vixen.

White men's sexual involvement with black women (even if it was rape) reminded white women of their subordinate position in relationship to him. White men could exert power to rape or seduce black women; yet white women were not free to rape or seduce black men. Although a white woman could condemn her man's sexual indiscretions with black female slaves, she was unable to dictate to him the behavior she desired. White women dared not retaliate by engaging in sexual intercourse with black male slave. From white women's response to black men today, it is obvious that the temptation was always there. Today, white women do not hesitate to engage black, desirable black men. It is hard to imagine this was not the case even during times of slavery.

White women directed their anger at their men to black women. It was inevitable that emotional ties developed between white slave-owners having sex with black female slaves. The white mistress would go through extraordinary lengths to punish black female slaves. White mistresses would use disfigurement to punish the lusted after black female slave. The mistress might cut off her breast, blind an eye, or decapitate another body part.

Hostility grew between black women slaves and white mistresses. White mistresses, living in comfort, were envied yet despised by black female slaves. White mistresses envied because of their material comfort and despised because white women felt little compassion for enslaved women's pitiful life.

There is still a lot of callous resentment between black and white women. If white women had done anything to change the situation of enslaved black women, her social position would have been jeopardized. Black women were inserted into the lowly position of laborer, which had been held by white women.

For years, white woman accepted black women being raped, accepted men and children sold on the auction block, and condoned children torn from the arms of crying mothers. The innocent children would be damned to a life of slavery, because the white slave father decreed it.

Today, many black women are probably more than curious about white women reconcile their ties the ancestral rape of black women. When white women stood by and looked on as black women labored under the burning sun in the rice and cotton fields, in the master's kitchen, hoeing land, plowing behind mule teams, what were they thinking? Black women are still curious how white women process their ancestral ties to the struggle of black women.

White women stood and watched black women perform back-breaking labor that was the domain of men. Black women, even today, are still curious how white women process ancestral ties in these crimes. She stood by, compliant with constant pillaging of black women's honor and heard the painful screams and cries of black women and young black girls being raped. Would she want the same atrocities perpetrated on her young daughters?

How do white men and women live with the guilt of the nightmare of black men and women being transported like animals on slave ships, where for every slave who made it through the voyage, one human being died? Slaves were packed below deck, "spoon-fashion," in minimum space. Wasting away in their feces, vomit, and flux, killed so many on this three-month voyage.

Above deck, the defenseless black women and girls were subjected to the most gross sexual abominations and perversions imaginable. The sick and dying were tossed overboard, while still alive, to the jaws of hungry sharks that had learned to follow the trail of humanity the slave ship left in its wake. How did white men and women then and today process the suffering of black people during this time?

Where was the white woman at the end of slavery, when white men continued to rape and impregnate black women and young black girls? White women were reluctant to and did not speak up in the defense of enslaved and helpless people. They were complicit in the mass spectacle of lynching that took the lives of untold numbers of innocent black men, women and children. Black's bodies were burned after being hung. Black men's flesh, charred and smoldering, was passed around as souvenirs!

What goes through the mind of white women, when she looks into the eyes of black women, knowing she has been spared the degradation that so many Native women, Black women, Asian women, and Latina women suffered so she can be placed upon a pedestal and leading a life of privilege? What really goes through the mind of white women when they look into the eyes of black women today and takes away black women's men in a manner other than lynching? A better question is what is going on in the minds of black men who permit such hurt to be perpetrated on black women?

CHAPTER 6

The Black Woman
(The Sick Rose)

There is never a time when I am not aware of my unworthiness to my female friends should I choose to view them as sexual objects. A man is a wolf in sheep's clothing, no more than sexual predators even under the friendliest circumstances. What is it about that statement that women cannot understand?

Each man knows that in the friendship of the lover there is no real kindness, he has an appetite and wants to feed upon his female friend. "Just as the wolf loves the lamb, so does the lover adores his beloved."

(Socrates, Notes on and Excerpts from Plato's Phaedrus)

O Rose, thou art sick,
the invisible worm
that flies in the night
in the howling storm

Has found out thy bed
of crimson joy
And his dark secret love
Does thy life destroy.

Blake, "The Sick Rose"

What a fitting analogy of destructive relationships between men and women. Some men diminish the tranquil lives of women just as the worm in Blake's poem sought to undermine the health of the rose while sheltered in the petals. The sexual impulse of men is second only to their love of life itself. How realistic are the wedding vows of fidelity? Women often underestimate the male sex drive. In the majority of men, the sexual impulse is the single most powerful motivation driving men's interaction with women.

In the privacy of your man's mind, it is conceivable that he has slept with all of your attractive female friends, your sisters and even your mother if they are slightly attractive. His sexual impulses frequently interrupt his most serious occupations throughout his day. Author Schopenhauer stated that, the dark side of men, "sexual impulses is the causation of the destruction of valuable relationships, the breakup of the firmest bonds, jeopardizes life and health through the contraction of sexually transmitted diseases, rob the honest of their conscience, make those who were once faithful, traitors."

Tragically, men's idea of falling in love with women consists of misinterpreting her motivations and thinking she is as sexually oriented as he. Misled by this perception, he abandons his own children and their mother for another woman who will indulge in his lustful weaknesses. Of all the delights in this world, sexual pleasure is very high on men's "to-do-list". Men are prone to risking fortune, character, reputation, and life itself for sex.

I mentioned all the above to establish the challenge with which all women are dealing. Black women truly do not have many viable mating prospects within her race. When black women, who are seeking a mate, encounter black men with women of other races, they struggle to free themselves from a sense of invalidation. Black women exchanging eye contact with White, Latin or Asian women, who are accompanying black men, understand that the statement being made by both is, "Yes, my sister you are invalid!" In this circumstance, black women simply look away and do not give the other women the pleasure of adding insult to injury staring them down in passing.

Jill Scott, a black female recording artist and actress, wrote an essay for *Essence* magazine where she expressed her dismay over seeing successful black men with white women.

> My new friend is handsome, African-American, intelligent and seemingly wealthy. He is an athlete, loves his momma, and is happily married to a White woman. I admit when I saw his wedding ring, I privately hoped. But something in me just knew he didn't marry a sister. Although my guess hit the mark, when my friend told me his wife was indeed Caucasian, I felt my spirit . . . wince. I didn't immediately understand it. My face read happy for you. My body showed no reaction to my inner pinch, but the sting was there, quiet like a mosquito under a summer dress.

> Was I jealous? Did the reality of his relationship somehow diminish his soul's credibility? The answer is not simple. One could easily dispel the wince as racist or separatist, but that's not how I was brought up. I was reared in a Jehovah's Witness household. I was taught that every man should be judged by his deeds and not his color, and I firmly stand where my grandmother left me. African people worldwide are known to be welcoming and open-minded. We share our culture sometimes to our own peril and most of us love the very notion of love. My position is that for women of color, this very common "wince" has solely to do with the African story in America.

When our people were enslaved, "Massa" placed his Caucasian woman on a pedestal. She was spoiled, revered and angelic, while the black slave woman was overworked, beaten, raped and farmed out like cattle to be mated. She was nothing and neither was our black man. As slavery died for the greater good of America, and the movement for equality sputtered to life, the white woman was on the cover of every American magazine. She was the dazzling jewel on every movie screen, the glory of every commercial and television show. She was unequivocally the standard of beauty for this country, firmly unattainable to anyone not of her race. We daughters of the dust were seen as ugly, nappy mammies, good for day work and unwanted children, while our men were thought to be thieving, sex-hungry animals with limited brain capacity.

We reflect on this awful past and recall that if a black man even looked at a white woman, he would have been lynched, beaten, jailed or shot to death. In the midst of this, black women and black men struggled together, mourned together, starved together, braved the hoses and vicious police dogs and died untimely on southern back roads together. These harsh truths lead to what we really feel when we see a seemingly together brother with a Caucasian woman and their children. That feeling is betrayed. While we exert efforts to raise our sons and daughters to appreciate themselves and respect others, most of us end up doing this important work alone, with no fathers or like representatives, limited financial support (often court-enforced) and, on top of everything else, an empty bed. It's frustrating and it hurts!

Our minds do understand that people of all races find genuine love in many places. We dig that the world is full of amazing options. But underneath, there is a bite, no matter the ointment, that has yet to stop burning. Some may find these thoughts to be hurtful. That is not my intent. I'm just sayin'.

The psychological damage to black women is just one part of the two-pronged assault on black women by black men. Her physical well-being is also imperiled by the insensitivity and selfishness of black men. Beset with one sexual psychosis after another, it is the promiscuous behavior of black males that harms the beautiful African rose's bloom. With rise of bisexual behavior of black males who choose not to reveal unchaste sexual practices encountered in prisons, and intravenous drug use, black women are being subjected to a greater danger of HIV.

HIV is now the fourth leading cause of death for black men and the third for black women. Blacks have seven times the new infection rate of whites, and the HIV-related deaths are highest among blacks (CDC HIV/AIDS Fact Sheet, August 2008). Black women risk contracting HIV each time she sleeps with a black man who insist on living a life of promiscuity. In doing so, the dark, secret love of black men not only betrays but destroys the life of the African rose.

Through all the violence and lynching, black women, were then, and remain, the foundation of the black race. The black woman is that "Rose" who is sick. Ironically, it is the black man who has become her worm of destruction. The black man has become the very same character he loathed in his white enslaver. He displays little resistance to what he views as harmless sexual escapades, especially when wealth and access brings him in contact with scandalous, opportunistic, sexy vixens from other races.

Opportunistic women of other races are more sexually motivated than black women. Once such a woman decides on a target blinded by desire, she does not hesitate to make the first move. When she makes that move, she communicates her attraction mentally and physically. Using her eyes and smile, she is alluring in her sensual hunger, leaving little doubt to her willingness to submit sexual favors.

She is very accommodating and wastes very little time. The difference between black and white women is that white women have more material wealth and are more free-spirited; they can be point blank about their interest in casual sex. Women of other races tend to be less financially challenged, and are usually fascinated about the sexual possibilities with a financially viable and virile black man.

Black women are not as forgiving of black men prone to infidelity. As their post graduate rates increase, black women have become competitive with white women financially, but many black women are reluctant to go after a black man who is not her financial equal. Unfortunately, many successful black men in metropolitan areas are dipping into the dating pool of women of other races. Women of other races, with different motivations, tend to be a bit more forgiving of the indiscretions of black men prone toward infidelity. It is as if these black men are disposable after a cruise or vacation, and where each is content satiating their sexual curiosity. After that, it's on to the next sexually stimulating black guy looking for sex without a long-term commitment.

In contrast, black women have different priorities for involvement. Many times, black men can attain material accommodations and sex from women of other races. In encounters with black women, black men may end up spending money and working very hard for sex with those women who are more interested in going to church and being saved, which makes them less free-spirited than white women.

Men find it stimulating and intriguing when endless possibilities are conveyed in ways that make it very difficult to misinterpret. When NBA Hall of Fame basketball player Charles Barkley (who is married to a white woman) was arrested for DUI in Arizona early New Year Eve's morning 2008, he told cops he ran a stop sign because he was in a hurry to get "oral sex." The former NBA star had been partying at a Scottsdale club with Michael Strahan (retired NFL star) and a bevy of beautiful white women.

According to the officer who wrote the report, "Charles Barkley told the officer he ran the stop sign because he was in a hurry to pick up the girl the officer saw getting into the passenger seat. The officer stated in his report that Charles Barkley asked him to admit that she was 'hot.' The officer stated that Charles Barkley also asked him, 'You want the truth? I was gonna drive around the corner and get a blow job.' Charles Barkley then explained that the woman in his SUV had given him a 'blow job' one week earlier and it was the best one he had ever had in his life."

I find it very interesting that for all their supposed beauty, women of other races are continually being cheated on by these black men. It reveals that these women simply are not providing something or there are psychological flaws in these black men that require sexual sedation.

I recall a (white) female friend who, after instructing me what to purchase at the grocer, came over to my apartment with a bottle of good wine and prepared a great dinner. Afterward, she suggested spending the night. Imagine, looking at her body through a soft, cotton sun dress, with nipples staring me in the face and the scent of wine on her breath, I thought that heaven must be like this. I saw no reason for her to go home and sleep alone that night. These circumstances just seem to happen more with white women than other female groups.

Sensuality becomes a greater priority for white women. With black women, men must provide the stimuli and coax her to do the things white women do naturally. There is no gate keeper for white women. Her passionate juices flow readily as they are easily stimulated by the forbidden fruit black men. Once white women gain access to what is forbidden to them, they take full advantage.

I cannot tell you how many times, I pass black women in the street, and they are very reluctant to be polite. They don't share a warm smile or even say hello. Many try very hard not to exchange glances. So, black women are not exactly friendly when they are approached; there is a lot of game that has to be sorted through with black women. Some white women are apprehensive as well. Culturally, black women have no excuse for ignoring black men when they encounter them. If a black man does "step out" with a white woman, black women who ignored him before, now, develop attitudes!

Black women tend to be more inhibited sexually. How significant are the inhibited approach of black women and the uninhibited approach of white women as each look for black men? Should modest sex be a deal breaker? A consensus, from the conversations I have had with many men, they are more accepting of uninhibited women.

Many black men need sex to affirm manhood. Sad but true. Many black men see women of other races as a sexy prize, open to sexual exploitation, that provides activity to be bragged about to close male friends as an ego-building exercise. The availability of oral sex can be a influential in a black man's decision to date black or white.

If black men could find attractive black women who did everything for him as white women, the possibility still exists that black women may still lose out. Remaining with a black woman prevents many black men from transcending the caste of being black in a historically racist society. Getting with a white woman remains an illusion of escape from a natural black existence complimented by a black woman.

Black women are visibly unnerved when they see black men with white women. That black man embraces his white friend, because she is submissive and takes care to explore his sexual interest. With most black women, oral sex almost never happens. Most black men actually appreciate the beauty of his black woman more, but the heightened sexual experience with his white lover leaves him feeling more treasured and appreciated. If all other things are equal, he often chooses white women, because they may be uninhibited about oral sexual activity.

Most black women will let a guy go down on her but her inhibitions will not allow her to go down on her man; black men appreciate his lover draining him orally. This is probably one of the most gratifying sexual experiences a man can come to know for more than one reason. This act is symbolic of the woman's complete attention to pleasing him. Black men rarely get this level of engagement from black women.

When a woman provides this kind of pleasure, it is empowering to the man in his relationship. He is motivated to cherish this unique combination of extreme passion and fealty in an amazing woman who is not one dimensional in pleasing him. A black man rarely experiences heightened, outside the box, pleasure with a black woman. From personal experience, white women have no problem stepping outside the box when it comes to sex.

When a man experiences oral pleasure, he treasures the powerful feelings awakened in him by such acts. If sex were a battle and explosive orgasms were heroic acts, his interracial lovers receive a chest full of medals for going beyond the call of duty. Black women, look at what is really happening. White women are literally sucking up to your man and running straight to the bank. Exhibit number one Tiger Woods.

Through these acts of sensual valor, interracial lovers are going straight to the banks with the money of many highly paid businessmen and professional athletes. Simultaneously performing oral sex on each other, or 69, is another act that influences a black man to prefer interracial lovers.

My black sisters, when you see your black brother accompanying his interracial lover and they are content while your stares bounce off them, like rocket-fire bouncing off the force shield of the *"Starship Enterprise,"* he is happy, because his white lover has taken him to the mountain. His sex life is like the exploding night sky on the Fourth of July.

Why are black women reluctant to venture beyond traditional sex in the bedroom? Black women may tell you that a history of sexual abuse and disrespect has collapsed her sensual priorities. Historical abuse by slave-owners and the resulting rage over that abuse has, in many ways, made her insensitive and uninterested in exploring her man's deeper interests.

Many women of other races have not experienced sexual and physical abuse on the same scale as black women. White women's approach to sex is totally different and originates from a spirit of being appreciated, whereas, black women operate as if some sexual acts are degrading. When black men encounter resistance in black women, the trait of promiscuity, conditioned in his bloodline by plantation breeding, is actualized, leading viable black men longing for other women who place a higher priority to sexual expressions.

The insensitivity of white men to white women, in typical relationships where the man works all the time and finds little time for wife; and the rejection of black women by black men creates the perfect conditions for black men and white women to come together at a very steep cost to black women.

As the landscape of wealth changes and pro athletes and business professionals select interracial mates as marriage partners, it is alarming that 42 percent of African American women are not married, and the higher their socioeconomic level, the less likely they are to wed. Statistics show only 5 percent of black women marry outside their race.

Between 1950 and 2000, the percentage of never-married black women doubled, from 21percent to 42 percent." The stat on the 2000 Census' show 42 percent of black women fifteen or older have never been married compared to 21percent of white women fifteen or older, for example, the number of black men choosing white women increase yearly after the Civil Rights Bill was passed in 1964.

Will black men continue to abandon black women? Will he desert the women who traditionally stood with him through thick and thin? Black men are you truly comfortable abandoning black women just to get your freak on with women of other races? You have gotten to where you are because of the strength, vision and love of your black mother.

CHAPTER 7

Black Men's Contribution to the Negative Reality of Black Women

How soon black men forget their history! Trapped within a postslavery ethnicity marked by racial violence, black men have stood on the shoulder of black women in order to move up in society. Black women have carried black men on their shoulders. They have supported him faithfully with hard work, while submerged in a tide of abuse, infidelity, humiliation, dehumanization and disrespect.

Now, with an agenda unrelated to freedom, black men are starting to reject black women as other races have exploited her wisdom and strength. How soon black men forget! In pursuit of sex with women of other races, lost to the generation of black men today is the history of mistreatment of black people by the larger societies.

Discrimination against black people is still alive and well. It is politically incorrect to voice what is truly thought of black people. The injustice now is manifested in unequal pay and unequal distribution of wealth. Also lost to black men, in promiscuous freedom, is awareness of how the role of black women as matriarchal ruler over the black family tribe is being quietly wiped out by AIDS, by genealogical displacement

63

through interracial relationships, and economically via mass incarceration of young black men.

Dr. Grace Cornish, psychologist and author of "*10 Good Choices That Empower Black Women's Lives,*" states "A lot of black men struggle to reach a certain level and they never feel they have reached the level of their white counterparts." Cornish continues, "They feel they need a white woman as part of that lifestyle. These are the black men who actually have a backlash against black women. They have not dealt with their own internal anger. Instead they see the opposite sex within their own race as the problem."

There is a psychological disorder called "dissociative fugue." This disorder seems prevalent throughout the rank of black men. It involves complete confusion over personality identity and often involves the partial or complete assumption of a new identity.

In efforts to be accepted in a predominantly white society, black men have the option to lose their black identity and take on an image that mirrors white values. Cultivating an image reflecting white values is the ticket to inclusion in a predominantly white society. Black people are reluctant to represent their black culture or even advocate black values for fear of being labeled radical or counter culture unless in that expression white entrepreneurs can profit from it through comedy routines, music, or athletics.

Many blacks, in order to assimilate into the larger society opt to surrender their cultural ethnicity. The conversion requires embracing the values of another race and the white standards of beauty. Accomplishing this has led to a new identity for black men that includes shunning black women.

For the black man, having sex with women of other races, can be a symbolic measure of revenge against white men and a measure of comeuppance. For black women, sex with white men is a constant reminder of the sexual humiliation she had to endure during slavery. Black women have a long memory and are not so trusting of white men's intentions. A black man's position in a relationship with a white woman will most likely be one of control. Black women find it difficult to warm up to a white man controlling her.

One critical trait that was bred out of black male slaves was the slave's development of a sense of confidence that he can protect and provide for his children. During slavery, a pregnant black woman was not protected by black male slaves. She was not pampered like the pregnant white woman. Sensitivity to protecting and providing for black women was bred out of many black men by the following realities: (1) black men had no control over the use of his woman's body; (2) there were other slave women he could sleep with during the pregnancy of his black woman; (3) black women were abused sexually by many men on the plantation, so it was a guess as to who the baby's father was; (4) after the slave baby was born, it could be sold away; so it was difficult for black men to bond with their children.

Having no emotional attachment to any child born of him helped ease the pain of seeing his child sold away. To this very day, the history of oppression, injustice and hardship experienced during slavery is re-enacted through each generation of black males due to the insecurities brought on by fear, uncertainty, self-doubt, and lack of control of his economic destiny. Such insecurities promote inclinations to bail out of relationships. This negative self-image from rare leadership opportunities erodes confidence in black males. For years, black athletes in the NFL were thought incapable of leadership roles as quarterbacks, because that position of leadership was expected to be provided by white men. Exclusion does a lot of damage to the development of the minds of black men.

Black men have traditionally used sex to deaden the pain of the struggle to rise above diminishment, injustice and oppression. Black men chase after women of other races for a sense of liberation, affirmation of his being, and for financial resources that sustain him in his quest to cut ties with a painful history mired in poverty. Slavery bred into black men an unnatural harshness and insensitivity that promotes the habit of dismissing his social obligations to black women and black children. This behavior is consistent with the mindset of black slaves on plantations, who were powerless to provide, guide, and protect.

In contrast, white males are taught from birth via the media and in everyday life by family, friends, and society that they are supposed to be leaders; they are the most valued people on the planet because, in their biased belief, that is the natural order of things. For white men, failure is not an option, and if they do fail, it is easier for them to get bailed out. The criminal justice system has been biased to criminal activities of whites as one expects in a government run predominantly by white people and for white people.

White men have centralized power in all institutions, which allow them to make the rules for others that they rarely live by themselves. White males are not taught that they are "in da club," they are the club with all the trappings the club has to provide. Membership has its privileges.

So, we have black males searching for affirmation and a share of influence in society while white males look to retain control of the institutions and retain their place at the top. Caught in the cross-hairs of the struggle of black men and white men are white women and black women.

Young black men are taught that they must be sexually aggressive, proud and self-assured. This is a tall order in a tough world where his skin-color and sexual prowess are two strikes against him fresh out of mama's house.

Like young black women, black men are also aware of social limitations and obstacles presented by white society. The thing that is not so obvious to a young black man are the limitations he places on himself by losing perspective of his history, and he becomes, obsessed with women of other races.

Because of black men's limited view of his own shortcomings, black mothers are beginning to instruct their daughters to expect to be left alone without a mate at some point in life. Just as many of their mother's mothers experienced abandonment, they must be able and ready to provide financially for themselves and any children they have.

Studies on the Hyper sexual Activity of Men

Black men are somewhat more active when it comes to sex than males of other races and much activity is dedicated to sexual predation. Young black men are enshrined in the macho club with the completion of his first sexual act and the loss of his virginity. The following studies provides indicators of black male sexual prowess.

Gonadotropin levels differentiate the races in the predicted direction and may underlie the difference in rates of multiple births. Testosterone levels may underlie other behavior traits differentiating the races, for they have been found to be 19 percent higher in a sample of black US college students than in their white counterparts (Ross et al., 1986). In an older group of US military veterans, testosterone levels in blacks measured 3 percent higher than Whites (Ellis and Nyborg, 1992). A study, of testosterone metabolites, showed a 10 percent to 15 percent higher incidence in black Americans than in white Americans and a still lower incidence in the Japanese in Japan (Hixson, 1992).

Rushton and Bogaert (1987) reviewed the literature on frequency of sexual intercourse. For example, Hofmann (1984) examined worldwide premarital coitus rates among young people in high school and found that African adolescents were more sexually active than Europeans, who were more sexually active than Asians. The same pattern has emerged from surveys carried out in the United States, where this pattern also holds for sexual activity after marriage. Rushton and Bogaert averaged data from a representative cross-cultural review by Ford and Beach (1951) and found that Oceanic and American Indian peoples self-reported rates of sexual intercourse per week ranged from one to four, US whites' ranged from two to four, and Africans' ranged from three to ten. Subsequent surveys support these data. For married couples in their twenties, the average frequency of intercourse per week for the Japanese and Chinese in Asia is 2.5 (Asayama, 1975; Bo and Wenxiu, 1992, table 7), whereas for American whites it is 4, and for American blacks, 5 (Fisher, 1980).

Racial differences also appear in measures of sexual permissiveness, amount of thinking about sex, and sex guilt. Abramson and Imari-Marquez (1982) observed that each of three generations of Japanese Americans showed more sex guilt than matched Caucasian Americans. In studies carried out in Britain and Japan, using a sex fantasy questionnaire, Iwawaki and Wilson (1983) found that British men reported twice as many fantasies as Japanese men, and British women admitted to four times as much sex fantasy as Japanese women did. By contrast, blacks reported not only having had intercourse with more casual partners but also with fewer feelings of distaste than did whites.

Rushton and Bogaert (1987, 1988) examined updated data from the Kinsey Institute for Sex Research (Gebhard and Johnson, 1979) that eliminated sources with known sexual bias, such as prostitutes. Black/white differences were compared on forty-one variables. For men and women, college-educated whites were found to be most sexually restrained, college-educated blacks least, and non-college-educated whites intermediate.

Sexual conquest is the rite of passage to attaining status for young men. "Real men" are those males who are virile, sexually active, and experienced. Consequently, for young black men, with higher testosterone levels, they seem to focus more on the sexual aspect of their lives and sadly preclude chivalrous rules on how truly to love in regards to him, women, and family.

In the absence of a male role model to contribute to the development of a chivalrous attitude in life, over-active hormones play the most significant role in black men losing themselves and the history of their race in the pursuit of women of other races who become easy sexual prey. I would again place Tiger Woods in that category. Institutionalized racism is a bit player in the ultimate demise of black men, but by far, black men have been their own worst enemy.

Black sexuality is sensationalized by the media. The hype in the media reinforces widely held ideas that black men and women are much more sexually deviant. Physically gifted young black men, caught up in the hype of hip-hop videos, are under self-imposed pressure to be sexually precocious as a rite of passage and requisite to being popular.

Fascination with sex has been a prevalent theme of black soul music. In present-day lyrics of hip-hop, many young hip-hop artists demean other blacks using the word "nigger." When the artists show no respect for their own through the use of the "N" word it becomes second nature to demeans women as bitches.

The lyrics of hip-hop music have made many young black men rich. Unfortunately, it sends subliminal messages that proliferates disrespect of black women. Black men's ability to dominate women sexually continues to be a panacea for lack of leadership and power, which black men experience in the larger society. Promiscuity continues to be the Achilles heel in the progress of black families. Such behavior is the product of a personality void of wisdom, self-respect, and knowledge of self. Men who are desperate to bolster a weak self-image and who are seeking external affirmation of others will resort to exploiting and demeaning women who are perceived weaker.

The emphasis placed on male sexual activity poses a direct problem for black men when approaching and entering into love relationships mainly because the "cult of masculinity" teaches men that satiating his sex drive is first and everything he does revolving around accumulating wealth has an ultimate purpose that leads to sexual conquest-but not necessarily responsibility to self and family.

While black women have yet to rise above their legacy of being exploited, devalued, and abused, white women have gradually made tremendous in-roads toward financial independence. The more independent a white woman becomes, the less committed she is to the concerns of white men. White women's resentment of the white men's agenda of total dominance can be seen in the rising trend of lesbian relationships and white women turning away from white male dominance. White women place less pressure on themselves when entering interracial relationships.

There are greater concerns than penis envy of black men for white men. With white women turning to lesbian relationships and interracial relationships with black men, white men are under seize by a two-prong attack from white women and the black men. Each black man seeks more power, status, rights, and liberation from white men's agenda to preserve his center seat in the world's power hierarchy.

The great black historian Chancellor Williams wondered whether the black race is lacking in one quality that seems to distinguish Caucasians and explain the reason for their long domination of the earth: their deep-seated concern about posterity, and the future role and welfare of their white offspring to the farthest generation. Their plans and policies

Of today's world are often based on expected outcomes centuries later.

Blacks, as a race, on the other hand, have been divided internally as a race focusing on good hair and bad hair, light-skinned dark-skin-issues, preoccupation with simply making ends meet, and keeping up with the Joneses. Simply put, blacks have lost their way and are not as far along in their process securing the future of their descendants. This matter calls for serious reflection, particularly on their race towards security with long-range planning whites.

In almost every period of history, we find whites carefully developing plans for their children's future. Though, none expect to see the plans realized in their lifetime, it does not stop whites from planting their seeds for future success. For many reasons, blacks have not taken the time to do so. Black men channel valuable resources into proving his manhood through sexual conquests. Divorces based on infidelity and babies born out of wedlock by multiple sex partners are testimony to lesser priorities.

In light of their long-term plans for their children, white men find the threat posed by the short-term sexually motivated agenda of black men troubling for his daughters. White men take many measures to prevent sexual contact between white women and black men. White men feel intimidated in one sense and threatened in another sense by reports about black men's physiques (large penis). This myth has generated curiosity and desire in women. Despite all of his wealth, the physical attraction and the intelligence of black men presents a formidable challenge for white men. So the exodus of white women to black men continues.

In reality, not much has changed from the days on the plantation where sex with black men and white women took place behind closed doors. The difference today is that there is less negative consequence for open displays of affection between black men and white women.

White women of today understand that black men are not the monsters they are portrayed as by white men. Truly tall, dark, handsome, and educated, black men are financially viable and very alluring to white women. White women are making themselves more accessible to black men. Each interracial relationship is a viable threat to the dreams and aspirations of black women.

Most white women I have encountered, who are open to interracial relationships, are aware of the side they are choosing in the black and white male power struggle. In the minds of white women, who are not socially conservative, there is some residual guilt over the unfair treatment of blacks. There has been very little discussion about what a cleansing experience it could be for white woman to make love to a black man. Having been intimate with several white women, I sensed some relief, sexual healing, and spiritual cleansing as perceptions of bias feelings were vanquished. It is almost as if white women seek peace in the intimate act itself.

My experiences with white women lead me to believe the sexual act has healing and spiritually qualities. I think because they are aware of the complicity of her ancestors in past race transgressions, it is liberating to provide sexual redemption. White men lack this compassion because of his fealty to greed, but the compassion is alive and well in white women. The act is more than physical pleasure.

The statement, "Once she goes black she never goes back," has nothing to do with penis size. It is the enrichment of white women's spirit through her interracial sexual experiences. She becomes committed to sexual diplomacy, thereby vanquishing racial tension.

When black men turn to women of other races, those women have a unique set of cultural and social agendas and use a black man's identity crisis and sexual addiction to advance them. Women of other races are far less likely than black women to challenge black men to focus on black history and the survival of black culture. Women of other races are black men's gateway from black culture into the larger society.

CHAPTER 8

Black Men Lost to Themselves and to Black Women

Women of color continue to battle oppressive and dehumanizing stereotypes, which no other women in society are forced to endure.

In America, blacks are a lost and divided tribe. Black Americans are disconnected from ties to an ancient and colorful ancestral African heritage of Kush, Nubia, and Meroe, which dates back to time immemorial. To make matters worse, the spirit of black men are stressed by constant struggle to the point where they shun instead of embrace black women. Because of black men's growing reluctance to protect black women, black women continue to be exploited in contemporary society just as Sara Baartman was in the early nineteenth century.

Amid the current confusion of black men losing self and identity, there is hope that exploitation of black women will end if black men find themselves and reunite in spirit, with black women, to confront racial bias and measures of social control by the larger society which continues to plague black communities.

The purpose of this book is enlightenment and to provide a platform of reason to launch new respect for black women from. Dreams and aspirations are fruitless without a foundation of wisdom from which to launch dreams.

Unenlightened black men are diverted from sensitive awareness of the plight of black women when their energy is, instead, directed to selfishness, obsessions with pleasure, and material wealth. Selfishness and superficiality breeds insensitivity. Insensitivity to virtue is the operating mode of the up and coming generation of black men.

It has become status quo for the so-called educated and prosperous black entrepreneurs and professional athletes to be arrogant, cavalier and out of touch with the struggles and challenges of black women. How can we awaken black men to the disrespect black women have been forced to endure?

The core of black women's problems with disrespect is associated with selfish acts of black men. The psychological scarring, induced by slavery to the culture of Africans males in America, has a devastating impact on relationships between black men and black women. It has been a strain for black men and women to develop as whole individuals while struggling with racial oppression. Starting relationships, with little knowledge of self, is a catalyst to producing unstable relationships and marriages. Psychological scarring is an important contributor to a negative outlook for black men, which they struggle with in relationships with black women. Without sufficient knowledge of self or well-defined goals on the part of both men and women, many black relationships are shattered early in their development. With so many failed relationships, it is difficult for black communities to sustain or refine cultural growth.

After a sordid existence of being bred like animals in slavery, bad habits of sexual infidelity, and being defined by his sexual prowess, promiscuous tendencies become embedded in the social mores of young black males, which erodes vital ethics needed to build solid family foundations in black communities.

So much of black men's energy is directed towards sexual conquest and his physical prowess that many have failed to develop as an equalizer to advanced education. Black men would do well to sublimate the energy invested in sexual conquest into post graduate degrees, becoming professionals in things other than sports, and creating wealth through investments to grow their savings. Instead of doing this, the priorities of many black seem to remain partying and womanizing. In doing so, they recycle bad habits and continue to undermine their relationships with black women.

Life is about seeking opportunities and making leaps of improvement, hopefully without hurting another in the process. By not continuing their education, which hinders upward financial mobility, black men are less able to support the needs and dreams of black women. By placing greater energy in promiscuous antics, black men cultivate a selfish mentality with little regards how the disrespect created through infidelity negatively affect the self-esteem, growth, and development of black women. Black men's selfishness and insensitivity creates a major dilemma for black women.

Black men are not the only source of trouble for black women. Black women continue to take typical crap from white superiors in the work place. Throughout the evolution of human history, people of different races have done terrible things to those of another race or creed. No race has a monopoly on ills and shortcomings because we are all human and do what humans do in moments of opportunity. We take advantage of weakness in others. This is very obvious in the work places where black women are very prolific but often are not rewarded for their productivity and leadership. They continue to receive the Saartje Baartman treatment.

Is there malicious will towards black women that prevents them from achieving their greater potential? This is debatable, as we continue to explore in this book.

Black men are betraying black women. Black men, especially entertainers and wealthy athletes, seem obsessed with pursuing sex from women of other races and pursuing sex with women for whom marriage is impossible (because of an existing marriage) or with women they have no intention of proposing marriage.

The list of black women not having men in their lives continue to grow, and their lives are relegated to metaphors of unfulfilled ambitions. It all begins with predatory instincts of black men.

Black male predatory instincts are misinterpreted as confidence by women of other races who are unsuspecting of the aggressive tactics of black men. It seems that an unending requirement of sex is a "cure-all" for anxieties of inferiority in black men, who historically have lacked leadership roles in cultures serving the interests of white males. It is as if black men's slogan is "if you are not permitted to lead in the business world, be a leader of what they prize the most and that is their women."

Aggression misinterpreted as confidence is a mask of insecurity worn by black men. Insecurity masked in aggression, at first, is seductive to women of other races who bite hard on the bad boy image. Desperate black men can be smooth operators. After the lies and deceptions, women of other races end up hurt and disappointed as well.

Promiscuous black men intimidated by strong black women, cross racial divides for women of other races and, in doing so, transitions black women from a crisis of dealing with infidelity to one of being deserted. Black women are in need of faithful, spiritually healthy, and virtuous black men.

What moral obligations if any do black men owe black women? In an age where global travel is common place, are black men free from the obligation as caretakers and guardians of black women? Some will say "yes, while" others say "no."

Very few black men are willing to accept responsibility for the estrangement of black women in society or even entertain notions of betrayal! Why should black men take ownership of black women's trouble when it is so much fun not to (can you hear me Tiger Woods)? As mentioned previously, a tremendous problem facing black families is the lack of a foundation. Undermining that foundation is a lack of sexual discipline in black men.

As black men rise from the ranks of financial mediocrity, their new found status and education place them in environments where black women's presence is minimal. A good example is the San Francisco Bay area where there are very few black women in the dating pool of black men. Black men are comfortable lost in the multi-cultural mix of white, Asian, and Latin women; in the Bay area, black men feel justified excluding black women from his choice spectrum.

In a totally different environment in Atlanta, Georgia, women are thought to outnumber men [2: 1]. Black women are well represented in Atlanta. Black men in Atlanta, who have financial access to women of other races, still prefer women of other races. So, to a certain degree, environment is a factor in black men dating other races of women. Beyond environmental factors, is there a deeper and more troubling issue with black men using women of other races for insecurity damage control? This is a powder keg subject, but there is an element of truth to the idea of the insecurity element influencing black men's decisions and choices.

Black men living in exclusive environments absent of a large population of black women still need to understand their contribution to the challenges and struggles of black women seeking mates. Being isolated and ignorant is not a very good excuse for men who understand what type of women he will encounter in the zip code of his choice. I honestly believe that black men would respond by selecting women of other races regardless of the environment. His choice is not determined by environment but by conditioned responses in his mind.

When it is all said and done, all black men, in either environment with or without black women present, are aware of the ramifications of their choices. They are simply servicing a disordered libido with a finger in the dike in a damage control mode of a perpetual image crisis.

Black women have a bit more game than women of other races; black women's defenses are a bit more challenging to break down. Black women certainly make black men work harder for sex, but access to black women is still there in each environment looking for a good man. Other women just make it easier for black men to get away with dishonesty and mischief.

Contact with other women naturally occurs as people of diverse backgrounds cross paths in school, on the job, and travel. An assessment of betrayal is not meant to indict many innocent black men out there who still honor and respect black women.

The mounting struggle that black mothers, wives, girlfriends, and daughters face in America exposes the growing disconnects between black women and black men. Dysfunctional relationship between black women and black men cripples the economic and psycho-social development of black families, communities, and black people as a whole.

Most black women's troubles stem from the choices of the man she loves. For many disturbing reasons, failing to secure physical and emotional security for their women and children, black men are in denial of their responsibility and are at crossroads of selfishness and unselfishness.

Losing fidelity and allegiance of black women is not a viable option for black men who are hell-bent on sacrificing spiritual and economic progress to cater to the adventures of promiscuity. Black women, more and more, find themselves without men in their lives and are feeling left out and abandoned.

It has become vogue for black men, single and fortunate even the not so fortunate, to change their image and shed traditional value of anchoring a black family. In the process, they are setting bad examples for the next generation of young black men. Black men are less concerned about abandoning their ethnicity than black women. Black women and their children are looked on as liabilities by many black men who are seeking an image make-over to secure women of other races.

Dealing continuously with racial upheaval and an image of inferiority, black men lost within white societies simply do not have the sensitivity and awareness needed to understand the current dilemma of black women. Blinded by lust and prone to infidelity, black men do not stand with his woman supporting her emotional instabilities. Nor have black men methodically cultivated the strengths of black women that would help balance and fortify her while she competes with other women in society and, at the same time, seek safety for herself and her children.

Collective goals of spiritual redemption, group respect, and greater prosperity could be realized by black people. By deserting black women, black men are complicit in destroying black communities, and ultimately the last vestiges of African pride in black Americans.

Anxiety over extinction has traditionally created tension and animosity between races. Black men are less vigilant of racial extinction than his White counterpart. The principles of species survival are very much in play in the mating game. The well-being and survival of black women are inversely proportionate to the survival of black people. Not concerned with the plight of black women, making decisions that set back the development of black communities, and ethnic heritage, black men expedite dissolution of black genealogy by spreading their sperm and wealth to women of other races.

According to reports, 6.2 percent of black grandparents are living with their minor grandchildren; that is twice as many as whites grandparents. Of these, half are responsible for the children's care. Approximately 1.2 million blacks (mostly women) are the primary caregivers for their grandkids.

What many black professionals and athletes fail to understand is that it takes tax money to build black communities. The first thing many successful black people do is move out of the community of their birth trying to keep up with the Joneses. While it may be unspoken, black men remain fascinated with having a white woman, and a black women with features such as those of actress Halle Berry that are very close to features of white women.

Bi-racial features or outright white physical characteristics such as a thin nose, blue eyes, or long, straight hair fulfill a certain image that many successful black men have. That image includes a certain type of woman who does not have traditional black features and life a neighborhood that surrounds you with white neighbors. The end result of successful black men and women pursuing such an image and lifestyle is destructive to improving the outcome of black America. We need the leadership of successful black men who give back to their black communities.

Black fathers should be mobilizing with black mothers to provide a quality education that trains young black children to discern between vice and virtue and that will help them make important choices in their lives as they confront their desires.

When it is all said and done, I understand that everyone is accountable for his or her success, failure, and ultimately, one's own happiness. Historically, black women have demonstrated a far greater understanding of the importance of "keeping it real and black."

In contrast to the efforts of black women, black men are defiant against uplifting their gift: "black Women." In whitewashing their lives by marrying women of other races and altering the genealogy of their offspring, black men do to themselves what they have fought to prevent other races from doing, which is to destroy black heritage and black pride.

Blacks in America are hard pressed to trace their ancestral roots. This is not a dilemma for other racial groups. Black men, in America, have no history to speak of except slavery. Through black men's struggles, black women have stayed the course during the hardest times imaginable! How do black men find it so easy to desert black women in selfish pursuit of a new identity with women of other races?

To this day, black women continue to be exploited and shoved in the background instead of given the same progressive opportunities as women of other races. It is a sin for black men to compound the stress of black women.

A robust discussion of why black women fail to keep black men by their side is needed if black women are to reclaim their honor and place alongside her man. Hopefully, such a discussion will trigger a renaissance of respect for black women and allow them to emerge from the shadows cast upon them by their own men and others in society.

What woman is more deserving as the mate of black men? Black women have definitely earned the right to a good life that can be provided by black professionals and athletes. Instead, the cream of the crop of black men is deserting the mother ship, "*Black Woman*," like the rats they are. Thinking with their penises, black men turn a blind eye as their mother ship, "*Black Woman*," goes down in the cold waters of neglect and indifference.

Just like many other black men, I have my personal war stories about relationships with black women. At the age of nineteen, I married my high school sweetheart, who was eighteen. There were sparks of love there that could have grown into a great flame. But the conditions in which I grew up did not instill in me the discipline required to make marriage work. There were no examples of creating wealth.

My mother was married to a good man with a big heart. He was uneducated and loved to chase women. My mom fought him and there were many nights when I would awaken to violent confrontations. My mom's struggle with an unfaithful man proved very disruptive to any ideas about longevity in a relationship. The deal breaker in growing up in an impoverished southern black household was not having anyone chart a path from the dysfunctional environment into college. The routine was to show up at school, play sports, float through my class schedule without ever thinking of challenging myself to make "A's" in my classes, huddle with my friends on the playground after school to play sports and try to have sex with a girl in the neighborhood.

This did not prepare me to deal with the complexities of marriage. It is amazing that after I graduated from high school and joined the navy; getting married was the first thing I decided to do. This was the first mistakes I made without the guidance of a father and no way of going to college. I was too undisciplined and immature to hang in there with a young and strong black woman and make a marriage work. I fell victim to the attraction of women of other races. Being wanted by them lifted me from a very unsatisfying journey in life. I got to act out a fantasy that seemed to be something out of Hollywood. Actualizing my fantasies and lusting after women of other races led to the failure of my first marriage to a very beautiful and faithful black woman.

Black women are sensitive and understand black men's endangerment from AIDS, disproportionate imprisonment, inadequate education, and brazen immaturity. Black women are forgiving of the shortcomings, but they are not forgiving of the disrespect that comes along with cheating. In the same light, black women are endangered as well. Black men seem not to comprehend fully the endangerment of his woman. Black men and women are in dire need of love, understanding and happiness. Sadly because of economic stress, black couples are intensively challenged to sustain the rare black pearl of love after they find it.

What can be said about the mental state and challenges of black men?

It is disturbing that black men continue to rely heavily on sexual sedation to medicate a painful psychosis of inferiority. This same immaturity of handling women also surfaces when some black men achieve wealth and act like a spoiled child.

The lesson many black men have not learned is that the measurement of success is more than making money or building a successful business. There are many men out there who are financially successful moneywise but they do not meet standards of high virtue, which distinguishes them as a good mate. Even with all their money, wealthy black men lost in a variety of psychotic aberrations, continue to demonstrate inferiority to their wealthy white counterparts. White men make it a priority to take care of their own. Black men export their wealth to other races by chasing sexual fantasies. Vilify white men if you will, but they do not abandon their women for black women on a large scale as black men!

Many black men, wealthy or poor, spend great sums of energy and resources pursuing women of other races. Is this black men's idea of equality with white males? This inferiority complex has extensive roots in the slave quarters, where, black male slaves fantasized about having sex with the white master's woman. And because he could not have her, a sense that he is inferiority was impressed upon the mind of the male slave. Fixation on the slave master's women was about being in control more than about sexual gratification.

By the choices of a growing rank of wealthy black men, it is evident the inferiority complex conditioned in male slaves is alive and well in the thought processes of contemporary black males. Black men have exchanged chains and shackles for validation games that promote a dark descent into insensitivity to black women and sexual enslavement to women of other races.

Women of other races provide the missing ingredient black women cannot provide that signifies true freedom and a form of escape in the minds of many black men. Black men in ego management damage control feel liberated from the negative stereotype of being black only when they are with women of other races. For a certain breed of black men, who are educated and financially well off, a black woman simply does not numb his anger and self-hatred like women of other races. In the minds of black men, riddled with psychosis and insecurities, only women of other races can provide an image make-over that would signify parity with white males.

Another group, demonstrating similar behavior of black men, is Asian women's pursuit of white men in order to gain parity with white women. Many Asian women, just like black men, are seeking affirmation by abandoning their culture for white men. Black men and Asian women are actualizing the same strategy as they seek status and affirmation.

Asian history is riddled with traditions of men women to unequal treatment. It is no surprise to see Asian women turning away subjugating from Asian men. Studies consistently show that Asians have the highest rates of intermarriage, and the Japanese are the most likely to have a white spouse. Those who are most likely to marry within their own ethnic group are Vietnamese men and women, Korean husbands and Asian Indian wives. Most Asians who marry a non-Asian have a white spouse; intermarriage with blacks and Latinos is less common. However, even among Asians, most people still marry someone of their own racial group. Twenty-two percent of Asian-American women have a non-Asian husband. A mere 9 percent of Asian husbands have non-Asian wives. (2000 Census Shows Interracial Marriage Gender Gaps Remain Large, March 14, 2003)

Eighteen percent of Asian wives have white husbands, while merely 7 percent of Asian husbands have white wives. The sex ratios of Asian/white couples are the mirror image of black/white marriages. Asian women have white husbands 3.08 times more often than Asian men have white wives. In other words, slightly more than 75 percent of white-Asian couples featured a white husband and Asian wife. However, unlike the situation with black/white couples, the gender imbalance is slightly less with cohabiting couples; only 2.09 times as many white men cohabit with Asian women as Asian men cohabit with white women. (2000 Census Shows Interracial Marriage Gender Gaps Remain Large, March 14, 2003)

Non-Hispanic whites marry other whites ninety-six percent of the time, with little difference between men and women in the rates of intermarriage (2000 Census Shows Interracial Marriage Gender Gaps Remain Large, March 14, 2003)

White men's persistence in disregarding and discrediting black women and their beauty is a manifestation of guilt. Acknowledging her noble qualities would mean taking ownership of a dreaded history and owning up to a racist motivated ugliness that runs deep to the bone.

The white man's deep-seated rejection of the black woman is an inability to confront deep-seated psychological flaws that compelled him to breed her like an animal and completely disregarding the humanity and beauty of black women as was the case with Saartjie Baartman.

Because of white men's position of power, they have been able to use economic tools to continue to deprive black women, and use these tools as leverage to preserve the same master privileges enjoyed during slavery. Black women are still under subtle unspoken pressure to submit, on the job to the white, male, dominant status, which from my personal conversations, many black women find stressful.

I find it very symbolic that actress Halle Berry was the first black woman to win an Oscar as a leading lady for the movie *Monster's Ball*. In it, she was a poor but beautiful black woman who takes on a white lover. Diana Ross was more convincing in Lady Sings the Blues. She was not awarded an Oscar. There are subtle subliminal messages of the formula of success for black women. Halle Berry's role symbolized the black woman accessible to white men who is open to violation. Diana Ross's character was less complicit and in love with a black man. There are so many subtle influences at work in shaping the behavior of the under-class of blacks in society. Many black have learned to play the game and are rewarded well.

Complicit to larger society's standards of beauty and highly educated, and earning substantial income, black men wastes no times checking into "Hotel Inferiority" and enrolling in the affirmation seminars of sex with women of other races. Sex with black women is just as exciting. The primary motivation for black men involved with women of other races is to dismiss black ethnicity by shunning black communities, avoiding black women, and even diminishing the number of blacks in their circle of friends.

Metaphorically speaking, in accommodating black men, black women have traveled with black men down long, dark roads in raggedy vehicles with bald tires, windows fogged with the fears, insecurities, and sexual dysfunction. The drivers of those vehicles have arrived on today's scene as frightened little black boys masquerading as men. Black women are empowered now and no longer have to ride in vehicles with frightened black men.

But even though they are empowered, some black women are content to faithfully remain a passenger in the raggedy vehicle. Black women have stood by her man, riding over bumps of racial upheavals and financial downturns. Why does she do so? Black women savor the sweeter soul fruit and a more complex paradigm of compassion in black men. When a black man has it all together, there is no better man than he. Not only black women, but women of other races appreciate the rare compassion of the soul of black men answering to a higher spiritual essence and they love the deep warmth of his soul's fire. This essence is why black women wait for a black man.

To her ethnicity, fidelity is the difference between the nature, courage, and discipline of black women and that of black men. Black men are no longer driven by the deep warmth in the heart of black women. The warmth and unique passion of black men, long cherished by black women, is becoming unavailable because of black men's inability to relate to his black essence.

Today, black men are too happy to abandon black women during a prosperity created by the struggles of previous generations of blacks who suffered racial violence and even death so black seeds would continue to grow. Is it too much to ask black men, upon reaching the mountain top, to bring black women so they can also breathe that rarified air of success?

As it stands, black women's dreams continue to go unfulfilled, and their hearts are reeling from the unrewarding long ride down the back roads in the raggedy vehicle with black men. The emotional devastation unleashed upon black women by the sexual dysfunction of black men has rocked her resilient, psychological core. The painful experiences leave black women battered, broken, deserted, and wondering what is really up with her black brother.

The strength of black women has persevered through unspeakable emotional and physical upheavals. She remains resolute on seeing her man safely through his search for equality. It is very disrespectful, if not painful, for black women to observe her man turn to women of other races. Black men's obsession with other women continues to play a huge role in damaging the esteem and derailing the social progression of black women. It also subjugates black women to continual humiliation and a degraded image of servitude. My mother toiled in this manner all of her life. Black women are goodhearted, warm, and loving. They deserve better.

Like Asian women looking to white men for opportunity and affirmation, black men see women of other races as the Holy Grail of affirmation. Many black men, weary from dealing with the psychologically trauma from dealing with racist environments created by the larger society, simply export anger and disrespect to interracial partners who are willing to forgive shortcomings black women are reluctant to accept. Black women's patience has run out and they are fed up with the excuse making, immaturity, and callous indiscretions of financially viable black men. All women have the same needs when it comes to relationships. All women seek fidelity. In having no respect for self, black men find it easy to disrespect their women, no matter what color they are. In the process of trying to overcome a multitude of challenges, it has gotten very complicated to be a black men rooted in deep love and appreciation for black women. To all black men out there, we must do a better job of taking care of black women!

CHAPTER 9

HIV AIDS Genocide Fact or Fiction

What are rap artists so stressed out about? Why are they so disrespectful to black women? The "rap culture" reminds me of dogs barking when something is making them very uncomfortable. Like nervous dogs that will not remain still, or settle down, rappers have an unsettled nature. Rap music reminds me of African war drums reverberating in the jungle in preparation for combat. Some people live in a moral dream world and some people are tuned into reality. Anger from black rappers comes from minds dialed into the reality of being black, poor, and disenfranchised in the ghettos of the world.

There are so many contradictory messages that our minds must filter. We live in a society that professes liberty and justice for all. Where is the justice, care, and real concern when impoverished and unemployed people are without basic health-care coverage? Why are there no cries of outrage while AID/HIV ravages sub-Saharan Africa?

The tandem of AID's assault on black women and the disproportionate incarceration of black men, who are bringing the AIDS virus to black women from prisons, ensures the decimation of black population in America. It is difficult to believe that a conspiracy to wipe out black people is not a reality when millions of African and people of African descent are disproportionately imprisoned or dying of HIV/AIDS.

In 2005, 2.3 million people died of HIV in sub-Saharan Africa. One person died every 13 seconds; 23 every 5 minutes; 274 every hour; 6,575 every day. The two things impacting the nuclear family of blacks is Imprisonment and HIV/AIDS.

- By 2008, 2,297,400 Americans were in federal and state prisons or local jails. Of that total, black men were incarcerated at 6.6 times the rate of white men.
- One in twenty-one black males was incarcerated at mid 2008, one in 138 white males were incarcerated. Black males (846,000) outnumbered white males (712,500) and Hispanic males (427,000) among inmates in prisons and jails.
- Of the 211,338 Americans currently serving time in federal prison, 57.9 percent are white, 38.5 percent are black, and 33 percent are Hispanics of varying race.
- Of those in federal prisons, 93.5 percent are men. 51.3 percent are incarcerated for drug offenses, versus 2.8 percent for homicide.
- Child deaths from HIV/AIDS in 2005 for sub-Saharan Africa alone numbered 520,000 for the world 570,000; and for North America 100.
- New child cases of HIV infection for sub-Saharan Africa 700,000; for the world 630;000, and North America 500.
- Children living with HIV for sub-Saharan Africa was 2.1 million; for the world 2.3 million; and for North America 9,000.
- Deaths from HIV/AIDS sub-Saharan Africa 2.4 million; the world 3.1 million; and in North America 18,000.
- New HIV infections in 2005 for sub-Saharan Africa 3.2 million; the world 4.9 million; and in North America 43,000.
- People living with HIV in sub-Saharan Africa 25.8 million; for the world 40.3 million; and North America 1.2 million

"Triple therapy" refers to combination of three antiretroviral drugs that help HIV-infected people live longer and healthier lives. In 1990-1992, the cost of triple-therapy for one person was $12,000. In the late 1990's, activist organizations in Africa and abroad launched drug access initiatives.

Protests were launched against pharmaceutical companies, demanding lower drug prices. In 1997, South Africa passed a law that permitted the government to (1) override drug patents and buy treatment at a discount from other developing countries or (2) allow production of the drugs by domestic companies. Pharmaceutical companies filed suit against the South African government, claiming that the 1997 act violated international intellectual property laws. Activist campaigns have accelerated around the world.

Countries such as Brazil, Thailand, and India ignore patent laws, and are able to produce drugs domestically for a fraction of the cost of those produced elsewhere. Brazil has been threatened by pharmaceutical companies and the US government, but it remains defiant. The end result is that pharmaceutical companies were forced to lower their prices. By 2003, pharmaceutical companies reduced the prices of drugs in the triple cocktails to less than $400 a year. This is a contradiction of principles of morality valuing money over human life.

AIDS is now the third leading cause of death for black women and the fourth leading cause of death for black men. Blacks have seven times the new infection rate of whites, and HIV-related deaths are highest among blacks.

From the Kaiser Family Foundation:

- Black women account for the largest share of new HIV infections among women (61 percent in 2006) and the incidence rate among black women is nearly 15 times the rate among white women.
- Black women account for most new AIDS cases among women (66 percent in 2007); white and Latina women account for 17 percent and 15 percent of new AIDS cases, respectively.
- Black women represent more than a third (36 percent) of AIDS cases diagnosed among blacks, while white women represent 15 percent of AIDS cases diagnosed among whites (as of 2007.)
- Although black teens (ages 13-19) represent only 15 percent of U.S. teenagers, they account for 68 percent of new AIDS cases reported among teens in 2007. A similar impact can be seen among black children.

Human rights activist, and HIV/AIDS advocate, and American lawyer Dr. Boyd Ed Graves spent two decades of human rights' work, judicial activism, and research on behalf of people living with HIV/AIDS. His work catapulted him into the world spotlight, earning him both international acclaim for his bravery and dedication as well as criticism for his controversial conclusions about the man-made origins and purpose of the HIV/AIDS virus.

Known by "Ed" to his friends and family, Dr. Graves was a dynamic and patriotic individual, who dedicated his professional and personal life to the disabled, disenfranchised, and the fair daily existence of men and women worldwide.

Born on July 7, 1952, in Charleston, West Virginia, to James and Theresa Graves, Boyd Ed Graves was the third of nine children. In 1955, Graves' family moved to Youngstown, Ohio, where his father and mother both worked several jobs simultaneously to purchase their first house. Youngstown would become Graves' home, and Graves would eventually become one of Youngstown's hometown heroes.

Graves began demonstrating leadership qualities at a young age, and after graduating Youngstown High School with honors as Senior Class President at age seventeen he was recommended by his Congressional Representative for an appointment at the US Naval Academy in Annapolis, Maryland. Graves was one of only thirty African Americans in the country to earn the honor. During his time at US Naval Academy, Graves learned Mandarin Chinese and was a member of the navy boxing team. Graves became the first African American elected as president of the US Navy Glee Club and was the first African American featured in US Navy recruitment commercials. At a time of extreme racial tensions and as one of the few black plebes, Graves was the victim of much hazing, harassments, and racial slurs inside the ranks. His experiences during this time were later featured in several books and articles authored by official US Navy historian Robert Schneller.

After successfully serving the country as a communications officer aboard the *USS Buchanan* as a Communications Officer, Graves left military life with honorable discharge and began his civilian career, entering the work force with IBM in 1977.

The civilian work-place echoed his military experience, and Graves, again faced with discrimination, and took the higher ground. In 1987, he successfully pursued a discrimination lawsuit and his appeals to the US Supreme Court. This was the first of several appearances in the U.S. Supreme Court Dr. Graves would make to fight discrimination for himself and others.

In 1992, Graves graduated with honors from Ohio Northern University School of Law in Ada Ohio, earning his Juris Doctorate During a routine physical exam several weeks before graduating law school, Graves tested HIV positive.

With his new diagnosis, law degree, and experiences as a minority, Graves went to work as a legal consultant, specializing in code compliance and enforcement for the Americans with Disabilities Act to ensure people with disabilities had equal access to facilities.

Determined to understand his diagnosis with a "new" disease, Graves immediately began researching HIV/AIDS, intent on understanding how to best preserve his health and help himself survive. In 1993 his research into HIV/AIDS led him to a formerly secret federal virus development initiative coordinated by the Pentagon called, "the US Special Virus Program."

"The Program" involved the complicity of two government agencies: the Pentagon as coordinator seeking bio-warfare solutions and the National Institutes of Health (NIH) as administrator. The cover goal of the NIH program was to meet Nixon's challenge of a war on cancer. Unfortunately for the program participants, the goal came at a cost of using humans / in vivo subjects to produce viruses, including the HIV/AIDS virus. For sixteen years, between 1962 and 1978, the NIH, published fifteen annual progress reports. Each year the report detailed thousands of human and non-human virus experiments and sought "candidate viruses." The most concise, salient, microcosm of this Mengele-madness was the 1971 US Special Virus Research Logic Flow Chart. The secret blueprint coordinates every experiment and contract inside the US Special Virus Program and demonstrates the true intent of the secret research—live human subjects, US citizens, US veterans, your brothers, uncles, cousins, friends, and neighbors.

On September 28, 1998, Dr. Graves filed his first class-action lawsuit in the Ohio Federal Court in *forma pauperis,* seeking immediate investigation into the formerly secret US Special Virus Program, including a petition to provide relief for the class of members infected by HIV/AIDS.

On January 1, 2000 the US Department of Justice notified Graves, they had named the Office of the President of the United States as the primary defendant in the case. On Election Day November 7, 2000, the sixth circuit federal court silently dismissed the case, Graves vs. the President of the United States. Graves appealed and on April 11, 2001, he appeared before the US Supreme Court. The court quietly dismissed the case without comment and with instructions "not to publish." Determined and armed with the 1971 Flow Chart, fifteen years of "missing medical history," and the evidence of the laboratory birth of AIDS, Graves continued filing litigation requesting immediate investigation into the formerly secret, tax payer-funded program until his death.

In 2001, Dr. Graves became the first American and African American to receive an injection of Tetrasil, the US Patented Cure for AIDS (Patent # 5676977). Almost immediately, Grave's health began to recover from years of damage inflicted by the "special HIV virus." He became an outspoken proponent of the Tetrasil treatment, demanding immediate clinical trials and worldwide accessibility for people living with HIV and dying of AIDS. Soon afterward Tetrasil, was recalled by the patent owner/ manufacturer, Dr. Marvin Antleman and Antleman Technologies, Inc., without public explanation. Graves took his experiences and requests to the Congress, General Accounting Office, the Centers for Disease Control and Prevention, United Nations, and the World Health Organization. He contacted, with varying degree of success, several Ministers of Health around the world, including China, the United Kingdom, and several African countries, where he was widely revered and respected as the "Man Who Solved AIDS."

Dr. Boyd Ed Graves was a celebrated lecturer and the author several books including *"STATE ORIGIN: The Evidence of the Laboratory Birth of AIDS"* and *"World War AIDS: The Third World War."* Dr. Graves was working on his memoir and other manuscripts at the time of his death. Additional information about Dr. Graves's life, accomplishments, and ongoing legal cases is widely available on the Internet. Dr. Graves's official Web site www.boydgraves.com, will continue on-line as a resource for readers who post news about the continuing legal work and, legacy, and as a method to allow others affected by HIV/AIDS to communicate, network, and contribute to his legal fund/endowment dedicated to continuing his life's work and.

The work of Dr. Graves and the war drums of hip-hop from the urban jungles is a warning to the transcendent and the mixed race, in their affluent slumber, that it is the assault on the dark-skinned blacks now, and it will be you next.

CHAPTER 10

Black Men Using Sexual Opiates to Cope with Social Rejection

Ecclesiastes 11:9-10 Rejoice O young man, in thy youth; and let thy heart cheer thee in the days of thy youth, and walking the ways of thine heart, and in the sight of thine eyes: but know thou that for all these things God will bring thee to judgment. Therefore remove sorrow from thy heart, and put away evil from thy flesh: for childhood and youth are vanities.

From a biblical perspective, men's use of women for sexual pleasure is looked upon from as evil. In the Ecclesiastes verse stated previously, God asks man to "put away evil from thy flesh."

Black men have created an image, for themselves, of the lover that masks great pain caused by the cross he must bear as a black man. Young, black men are unaware that their image of the lover masks the pain of struggle against injustice and unequal treatment in society.

Black men's fascination with, lack of discipline regarding, and sacrifices for sex reveal his pain, no matter what extraordinary lengths he goes through to hide it. It is fascinating how the release of addictive components prolactin, oxytocin and vasopressin during and after sexual intercourse slowly establishes controlling influences in the minds of young males.

Prolactin, which is released after sex, acts as a sedative. Oxytocin and Vassopressin are other chemical agents that help couples bond after sex. Black men from dysfunctional homes seek happiness and security not found in their family environment, and these post-coital, naturally occurring chemicals can make them feel they have found happiness and security.

The brain has a reward system designed to make people and other animals do what they ought to. Without it, they might forget to eat, drink and have sex—with disastrous results.

Animals pursue sex because sex makes them feel good. They feel good because of the release of dopamine into the brain. As mentioned previously, sex also stimulates the release of vasopressin and oxytocin in people and they feel good too. Parts of the brain that are love-bitten include that part responsible for gut feelings, and the part that generates the euphoria induced by drugs such as cocaine.

So the brains of people deeply in love do not look like those of people experiencing strong emotions; they look like the brain of those snorting coke. Love, in other words, uses the neural mechanisms that are instrumental in the development of addictive behavior. "We are literally addicted to love." Helen Fisher, a researcher at Rutgers University and the author of a book on how we love, suggests that love come in three flavors lust, romantic love, and long-term attachment.

Lust, of course, involves a craving for sex. The aftermath of lustful sex is similar to the state induced by taking opiates. A heady mix of chemical changes occurs, including increases in the levels of serotonin, Oxytocin, Vasopressin and endogenous opioids (the body's natural equivalent of heroin). "This may serve many functions, to relax the body, induce pleasure and satiety, and perhaps induce bonding to the very features that one has just experienced all this with."

Then there is attraction, or the state of being in love (what is sometimes known as romantic or obsessive love). This is a refinement of mere lust that allows people to home in on a particular mate. This state is characterized by feelings of exhilaration, and intrusive, obsessive thoughts about the object of one's affection.

Wonderful though it is, romantic love is unstable and—not a good basis for child-rearing. But the final stage of love, long-term attachment, allows parents to co-operate in raising children. This state, says Dr Fisher, is characterized by feelings of calmness, security, social comfort, and emotional union.

Because they are independent, these three stages can work simultaneously, with dangerous results. As Dr Fisher explains, "You can feel deep attachment for a long-term spouse, while you feel romantic love for someone else, while you feel the sex drive in situations unrelated to either partner." This independence means it is possible to love more than one person at a time: a situation that leads to jealousy, adultery, divorce, and to the possibilities of promiscuity and polygamy, with the likelihood of extra children, and thus, a bigger stake in the genetic future. As Dr Fisher observes, "We were not built to be happy but to reproduce."

Unfortunately, unequal distribution of wealth and, other social inequities, along with a legacy heavily stained with promiscuity during slavery, has created a form of dementia in the psyche of black men. In this psyche, is the propensity for abuse, reckless disregard for himself, and an indifference to the outcome of his people as a race.

Front and center of the dilemma of black men is the problem alluded to by Dr Fisher "Black men's lust for white women stems from the absence of the desire for deep-seated attachment for a long-term spouse, which causes him to steer clear of what black women want."

Excessive conditioning to unbridled sex in the slave quarters cultivated independence that permitted feelings of romantic love for one woman while feeling sexual attraction for another. Black men were raised in a culture that encouraged promiscuity. Black men have a deep-seated notion that they can love more than one woman at a time.

Black women have a reputation of being aggressive, and; much of their behavior has been conditioned by the behavior of promiscuous black men. At the heart of the problem of the black nuclear family is the black man's obsession with multiple sex partners.

CHAPTER 11

Differing World View of Promiscuity Between Black Women and Women of Other Races

Some white women openly admit what they want from black men. One white female wrote,

> Black men pursue me. We look at one another and express longings for passionate sexual energy in the lingering glances. Our attraction is based first on the differing physical attributes of race. We are not those couples who "happen to fall in love." "We are of a different breed of lovers and purposefully come together out of some greater need to explore the forbidden fruits in search of greater understanding and respect of the racial differences that has kept us apart. This union is not politically-correct.

The Internet has made it a lot easier for black men and white women to find each other. Black Men advertise, "Ebony seeks ivory. "White women write, "Seeking tall, dark, and handsome; very dark." We are not the same people who say race is not important. It is important to us. We have race-specific desires. Another woman wrote, "Black skin is thick and lush, sensuous to the touch, like satin and velvet made flesh. There's only one patch of skin on a white man's body that remotely compares to nearly every inch of a black man's skin. WOW! The first time I caressed black skin, it felt like a luxury I shouldn't be able to afford."

A white woman past forty is often passed over by her white male counterpart. She goes younger, ethnic, foreign-born, down the socio-economic scale, darker, or she spends lonely nights at home with her cat. Black men are happy to get the babe they couldn't have when she was twenty-something and fertile. That's a lie.

The truth is mature white women attract about the same percentage of available white men her own age bracket. There is an abundance of white men available to mature white women where celibacy isn't a factor. However, many white women do not want less than an athletic white lover.

Black men have more energy, style, and edge in comparison to their white male counterpart. Black men understand the art of flirting, a nearly lost craft by white men obsessed with wealth and power. A black man is so damned sexy, and he knows how to make a woman feel special and attractive.

Black women are furious, after the brutal history of enslavement, that black men are still vulnerable to a different kind of bondage by white women, which is sexual bondage.

Many white women admit they are after the sex, not the ring, and black men aren't the marrying kind anyway. Yet, black men continue to choose the women white men reject. At the same time, he is abandoning his beautiful African princess, who needs him dearly. Women of other races who go after black men are in heat. According to one school of thought, white women turn to black men when their sex drives kick into higher gear and their social inhibitions recede.

White women are getting the opportunity to discover the attractive attributes of black men as he is beamed into homes throughout America on television. In baseball, football and basketball, black professional athletes are marketed much like a gladiators with a daring swagger, rippling muscles, competitive and fierce personalities, and they are financially viable. The not so gifted black men are motivated to follow the lead of the super-stars and attempt to get in where they fit in. When the average black man copies the behavior of professional athletes, problems can ensue. And this behavior is bad news for black women.

White women understand that there is nothing to stop them from experimenting sexually with black men who they discover are confident, masculine, and sexy. White women are aware that black men can be gentle and far from being monsters.

Dominated by political and financial concerns, white men have not been sensitive to the needs of white women. When black men turn on the charisma, it makes neglected white women feel sexy, wanted, respected, and desired! It is refreshing, stimulating, and risqué for a white woman to let go of her inhibitions with a black man.

It is interesting that black men targeted by white women are viewed as not the marrying kind. It reveals a disturbing attribute of many black men in that they lack discipline and self-control when it comes to sex. This flaw in many black men's character is his Achilles' heel. Many black men credit white men with creating inequities that serve to keep him oppressed and in bondage. That may be true to a certain extent, but with little discipline to counter-balance promiscuous tendencies; black men create their own prison.

White men may be guilty of placing drugs into neighborhoods. With discipline, black men could avoid the destruction by choosing not to get involved with drugs. When drugs are introduced to individuals who lack discipline and have very little control of his sexual urges, you can sit back and let natural destruction take its course. Marriages will not be pursued, marriages that are made will be broken, women and children will be abandoned, education will be forsaken, and generations will be derailed into obscurity.

The greatest sources of destruction in black communities are drugs and lust for women of other races. Historically, drugs and women of other races have the same impact on the black communities, which is removal of black men and the destruction black men's fidelity to their culture, family, and environment. If a woman of another race just happens to find a black man who is the marrying kind, one more black man is uprooted and transported to white communities. Viable middle-class or transcendent black men who follow the lure of women of other colors to non-black communities leave single, black women with the less than desired, typical, promiscuity oriented, players, and hustlers.

The outcome of a sexual relationship between a black male and women of other races, being what it may and bringing to the table what it does, is a co-dependent relationship where, during their sexual encounter with black men, women of other races transcend traditions, which had sheltered her from so many truths. Engaging black men actually free white women from the pedestal onto which she has been placed.

Once out of that cage, women of other races are enlightened by her dark lover. Unlike her experiences with other men, white women's experiences, with black lovers, complete them physically and emotionally. See the Kardashian sisters' involvement with Ray J, Reggie Bush and Lamar Odom. Black men, so erotic and electric, literally prick white women's pseudo-pristine bubble with an emphatic pop. Some white women use the analogy of Porsche to a Volkswagen to describe the difference of making love to a black man, compared with other men.

How do black men stem the drain of child support payments on his financial resources? The impact of directing financial resources to undisciplined sexual adventures prevents many black men from investing those same resources into the stock market. Black men need a more-disciplined, goal-oriented approach to socio-economic development. This has to start in the home with a father and mother acting responsible to the fruits of their union.

Many relationships are established on sexual attraction. Unfortunately, many black men, unwittingly it seems, are dependent on women to release dopamine properties in the brain that make him feel good about who he is, instead of deriving satisfaction from disciplined principles based on respect for self and the women that are exploited sexually. It comes across as cute, but a lot of damage is done when so-called innocent sex leads to pregnancies or worse, HIV/AIDS.

A safe and secure home life with committed loving parents is vital to the image make-over for young black males. Because of the hardships encountered in their lives because of, slavery and racial discrimination, many black men have gotten discouraged with religious dogma. For many black men, their belief has been tested to the limit and their faith has been relinquished for worldly short term-gratifications. The belief in marriage has been tossed out with the wash. Because of this, the institution of marriage is not as stable as it should be. Marriage introduces a greater struggle and challenge many black men feel is too much of a burden when it coincides with racial discrimination that prevents him from making the same money as many white men.

With the decline of the two-parent household, many young black men are left with struggling mothers doing their best to hold together a broken home. If the anguish of not knowing the strength and protection of a strong male role model was not a dominant presence in the psyche of young black men, they would be less inclined to use sex as an opiate to sedate the depression, anguish, and pain of growing up in a dysfunctional home.

In many cases, it is somewhat understandable that adolescents are clueless about who they are. It is really sad that older, experienced, black males have not advanced beyond an adolescent image crisis. Psychological counseling is a possible solution but the patient has to be aware he is sick and voluntarily seek help. Herein is the problem: black men are not aware of their ongoing psychosis that renders discipline inaccessible and promotes promiscuity. Though many black men need psychological counseling, many do not have access to health benefits that would provide access to mental health facilities. Free health care for everyone is something that should be provided by the larger society, especially when its black population has the trauma of slavery embedded in its developmental path.

One great outcome of religion is that it instills discipline. The downside to religion is that the response to religion can be a mechanical one. Religion can be a much more powerful force in the lives of people if ministers in the mega-churches actually exhibited examples of frugality, avoided scandal, and led a life that does not contradict messages of humbleness.

Black men would respond to other successful black men who have achieved a modicum of success and voluntarily reach back into the black neighborhoods to help and show those struggling a way out. When other successful black men start giving back, it gives religious messages teeth and promotes actions people can see that inspires them to believe someone loves and truly cares for them. When ministers of mega-churches are inaccessible in their gated communities, Lear jets, and Bentleys, along with molesting young children, responses to religion will be mechanical.

I advocate men to act from knowledge based on a respect for self that naturally promotes love and respect for others. This is love from the heart and is not instilled via religious dogma. If this love and respect are not possible, religious dogma is the next best thing.

Our culture promotes personal drive, competition and greed. Personal drive and competiveness evolve into psychosis when we use greed as a reason not to care for each other. This psychosis is embedded beneath all the other insecurities of people who design identities based on wealth. Women are guilty of forgiving men's dysfunctions if he has sufficient income to provide a perfect cover for his personal shortcomings. It is a shame that women reward men's shortcomings if men are wealthy. If women of the world united, much of men's bad behavior could be changed. Why are women so forgiving? They are so forgiving because they are also enslaved to their own dysfunctional images that are dependent on material wealth.

Men and women prey on each other relentlessly through altered images and lies. We have incorporated deception as a norm in our relationships. Each of us markets a unique idiosyncrasy of deception, going from one relationship to another, shedding one image after another, and moving out of one cycle of deception to another one with a different person.

To advance beyond cycles of dysfunction, it is necessary to see yourself caught up as a knowing and willing participant in multiple schemes of deception. We are all perpetrating some image and are all looking for validation. To get beyond the need for external validation requires loving yourself via self-validation.

The image thing is used much like a fisherman uses a lure to catch fish. We need an image that brings attention and reward our way. Our greatest troubles come from people we attract with lures of uncertainty. This occurs mainly because we need others to mask uncertainty and fill a void created from a lack of self-knowledge. It is not enough for us to love ourselves; we need validation from external resources to feel whole.

These insufficiencies of self-love and self-reliance turn each of us into predators, like lions looking for their next meal. A life based on the pursuit of pleasure is often a painful experience, leaving broken hearts and unhappy outcomes.

Seeking affirmation is painful and creates ongoing conflict. We are always surprised when no one sees us quite the same way we see ourselves. When you tell the one you love that you love him or her, you are complimenting an image of who you think that person is. In the end, after disagreement, conflict and eventual break up with that person, we often find the image you loved was only real to you for that moment in time. To survive in love is to be an open receptacle of many images of a changing person to come. The greatest problem in relationships is trying to hold onto a rigid image of a person and not embracing change. This is an extremely painful process because of the insecurity created by the uncertainty of the unknown as to what your loved one is capable.

Men are simply junkies to the natural chemicals that are unleashed in their brains during sex. The chemical addiction is powerful enough to make black men destroy their most valuable relationship with black women.

Are black men truly traitors to their women? Is treason a fair assessment of their actions? I think neither. I think the struggle of social inequities has produced a group of depressed men that uses sex as an opiate for pleasure to counter the pains of their struggle to overcome broken homes, lack of love, and racial inequities that have produced unhealthy mental complexes in the minds of black men.

Until the conditions that promote stress are removed from his environment, treachery, deception, and infidelity will remain black men's calling card for all women. Simply put, black people need the strength, guidance, vigilance, and reinvestment of the few successful black businessmen and athletes, in black communities. When the wealth earned by black men is not reinvested into black communities, the larger society benefits, while black neighborhoods go under.

Unfortunately, in order for financially successful black males to assimilate into the predominant white mainstream, as many desire to do so, they relinquish their culture by turning from black women to women of other colors for wives and family.

An argument can be made that, from a psychological perspective, black men are extinct. In terms of psychological perspective, there are very few real black men left in countries outside the continent of Africa. In the process of marrying white, the features of black babies continue to undergo genetic alterations. Through the process of neglecting black women, black men make down payments to the destruction of black civilization and any hopes of redemption of black people as respectable in the eyes of communities around the world.

Regardless of the method by which other races have chosen to secure wealth and power, white societies are very deliberately attempting to preserve their roots and to take care of their women and children. If historically the wealth and power of white societies was produced at the expense of an under-caste of black men and black women, today is a different time for black people. We cannot use naïve innocence as an excuse anymore.

Some control has been given to black people to move away from the negative stereotype produced by the legacy of slavery. Black women have the right idea on how to accomplish redemption, but cruelly, black men are willing to throw black women under the bus for women of other races.

In America, black men continue to drift out of touch with America's history of injustice toward blacks. As they drift, black men abandon dreams of many slaves who struggled, suffered, and died so contemporary black men would have the chance to raise black children. Black men seem eager to desert their communities and women for the mercenary principles of capitalism. No matter how financially prosperous, no matter how many home runs they hit, touchdowns they can score or basketballs they can dunk, black men, are spiritually broken and mere illusions of the once-proud African warrior.

Truly enlightened and courageous black men like Martin Luther King Jr. are very rare. The instinct to stand up for virtues and principles has been bred out of contemporary black men by lust and greed. For years, black men were conditioned into helplessness by being forced to witness the violation of his women and children at the hands of the larger American society. To this very day, young black men are still not free as they are incarcerated on a massive scale by a corrupt criminal justice system.

There is no fight left in the black man for his struggling brother, dignity, his woman, or challenges of young black boys and girls. While black men find comfort in the illusion that he has escaped his ethnicity by choosing women of other races, black women suffer in stunned silence.

Women of other races are content to give black men a break from black cultural obligations. On the other hand, strong black women are not so quick to indulge black men's selfish pleasures and demand better ethnic ethics from him. Because of commitment to her cultural ethics, black women are being abandoned.

Black women are concerned about the outcome of developing black men as whole individuals. She wants a healthy and prosperous outcome for her family and she wants a fair chance for her children to compete for leadership roles in society. Developing the appropriate attributes for success requires commitments and ethics that growing ranks of unenlightened black men have been unable to discover or pass on to their children.

Black men in relationships with black women can be compared to taking a more-demanding class in ethnicity while black men being with women of other races is like taking a sex education class. The course given by black women requires discipline and commitment. Black men are flunking the black women's course at alarming rates.

Responsibility and discipline are not a requirement in sex education classes by women of other races. Home work is minimal and many times black men do not even have to attend class. While stimulating physically, in relationships of a sexual nature there is no real kindness. It is just two people with a physical appetite feeding off each other. It is often a mutual decision that neither black men nor women of other races look for long-term gratification from their unions.

Choices reflect individual's unique requirements of affirmation. For some black men, only women of other races will serve as the source of affirmation.

The need to control is a strong characteristic that drives sexual addiction plaguing black men. Living under oppression, racial segregation, and bias has devastated black men's psyche, and many black men are oblivious to the depths of that damage.

Sex is the panacea to all that afflicts the oppressed. Black men, have not found another outlet for all their frustrations and the resentment of how they've been mistreated while struggling to overcome racial oppression. Sex with women of other races remains the opiate of choice of black men; it is an intoxicating drug in itself. I think way too many black men are fixated on the dopamine rush achieved from sex.

The Dehumanization of enslavement and living according to the opinions of others has created a spiritual imbalance in the psyche of black men. No matter how much wealth black men accumulate in America, because they are spiritually broken, they will remain lost to the sense of purpose exemplified by the likes of Martin Luther King Jr., Thurgood Marshall, and Malcolm X.

Black men have fallen into the same trap as white men; neither are not truly happy, so pursuit of happiness has become a race for more wealth and opulence. Black men, and men in general, are on pointless, empty journeys, and being in unfaithful and rocky relationships with men and women alike reflects the flaws in the core of the spirits of all people. Because of these flaws, people find themselves obsessed and controlled by short-term physical aspects of being instead of developing deeper long-term spiritual bonds.

In sexual relationships between black men and women of other races, it is a clash of predators, each preying on the other. Often, black men who prefer women of other races are busy and distracted from commitment, preferring to have several lovers and take advantage of the permissive nature of women of other races.

Women of other races have other social distractions and commitments that cause them to invest minimum energy in keeping tabs on her black lover. Black women are more vigilant of black men's indiscretions and will not permit precocious black men the same promiscuous freedom, as do women of other races. Black women, refusing to be disrespected, are demonized, because she is not willing to compromise the need to be honored and respected by her man.

With a liberal mind-set and complete understanding of the promiscuous nature of black men, women of other races are eager to indulge the weaknesses of sexually motivated black men. Black women, however, are looking for respect and commitment backed by virtuous qualities. By providing easy access to sex, women of other races undermine black women's efforts to end the promiscuous habits of black men.

Sex is a coping mechanism for much of the trauma black men create through deception and promiscuity. Dependency on sexual highs robs black men of spiritual vitality. For too long, black men have used sex as a crutch. He uses sex in as a junkie is strung out on drugs. Like a junkie who cannot clean himself up, while still using drugs, men cannot improve their lives if the energy and time lost through sexual addiction is not replaced with more virtuous and ethical priorities.

Sex is used in relationships the way an artist uses paint to create a masterpiece. We are all artists at heart. The canvas is a friend or spouse we choose as a sexual partner. Relationships are art projects that can be finished in a short period of time, where we find ourselves jumping in and out of bed with different partners. Or it can be a long-term masterpiece with one life partner. Orgasm is the emotional paint that brings color and definition to the portrait of love.

Most people are very passionate about their emotional art work and offended when their mate is working on more than one project at a time. An emotional artwork of love depends on honesty for refinement and rich colors for definition. Dishonesty is much like trying to paint a portrait when the model keeps shifting positions. You cannot capture the true emotional essence of love unless the model of love you are trying to capture remains still or committed through sex, we can enter into a private and deeply intimate realm of trust and regard. The essence of a person is physically personified in their sexual expression. Sex is that interpersonal cross-road, where the spirit and energy of two people meet to become one exquisite work of art.

When a woman gives herself to a man, there is nothing about her left unexposed. Otherwise, without the sexual encounter, heterosexuals have to be very creative to maintain more than prurient involvements with women. Men use intimate access to control and break down a woman to serve his selfish desires. This is why sex is so important to men!

Men are selfish and sex is a drug to them. They have many women, just as a junkie has many places to stash his drugs. It is critical to a woman's happiness for her to know whether she is being used as such. Black men and women of other races have a similar sexual addiction. Black women tend not to cooperate with the promiscuity of black men, while women of other races put up with it. Because they are usually more financially secure, women of other races concentrate on sexual pleasure, while security and commitment are exceedingly important to black women.

Black men's fascination with their libido creates a spiritual imbalance within their psyche. This imbalance drives many black men to women of other races for sexual pleasures. It also leads many to a life of drugs and alcohol and obscures intellectual depth perception and an ability to understand he is being systematically deconstructed through mass incarceration, HIV/AIDS, and by his own choice of women he to bear his children.

Many black so men are sedated with the opiates of sex and intoxicated by acquiring small parcels of celebrity status that they abandon their women and no longer stand for anything. Black men should wake up, kick their sexual addiction, and pay attention to what is really going on today.

I lived in Northern California in the seventies and eighties and there was a fairly significant population of blacks in the San Francisco Bay area. Today, I infrequently see black individuals in vehicles on the expressway outside of the Oakland area. It appears the cost of living has caused many blacks to leave the area. I wonder if the disappearance of blacks, such as what is taking place in the San Francisco Bay area, foreshadows what is ahead for blacks in America. With the AIDS epidemic killings millions in Africa each year, what are the prospects for the future of black people worldwide?

CHAPTER 12

Advancing Beyond Cycles of Dysfunction

It is important for each of us to understand how our individual micro-fragment of dysfunction contributes to the macro-cultural dysfunction. The world is each one of us. Our society, the culture that conditions us, is the result of the individual s experiences of happiness, sorrow, envy, and compassion. Each one of us is a component of the overall cultural soup. The sad thing about humanity is that we wait until catastrophic events before the natural instinct of love comes forth.

Each person exists in a little cocoon, with selfish goals that limit us in relating to each other through our fears, biases, and worldviews that rarely are fashioned from ideas borne of clarity. Many of our traditions are mired in distortions created through the cultivation of greed and pursuit of pleasure. Each person's ambitions are shaped by traditions and values that promote objectifying those perceived different.

People fail in their relationships with each other because they communicate through images, which prevent them from establishing a relationship based on who they really are. Everyone is obsessed with looking and acting successful by the clothes they wear, the car they drive, or even the college they attend. It is very peculiar the image many young black men have taken to. They wear big baggy shirts and pants that hang off their butts with underwear showing. The young men I observe wearing their pants in such a manner are locked into a counter-cultural mentality. From broken homes and tough neighborhoods this identity brings attention to a person who feels he has not been embraced by society. You can say it is the costume of the disenfranchised.

Wearing baggy pants hanging off their butts is a way for someone who feels forlorn in deteriorating neighborhoods to invalidate anyone who does not dress with hardened ghetto flair. The image of the baseball cap worn backward resonates the same way. Everyone perpetrates an image, whether it is baggy pants, Oakley shades, or riding in a sleek BWW. The point is that we are all lost in the images of baggy pants and BMWs.

Images are transitional and forever in a state of flux, so it is very difficult to know who and what we are from day to day.

The rich are different from you and me. They're damn well positioned to keep oppressive measures in place, and damn anyone who seeks ethical forms of justice in the political arena or economic market place. In the state of Florida, the governor is a millionaire, eighteen of forty state senators are millionaires, and thirty-four millionaires vote in Florida's house of representatives. In 2009, according to the Center for Responsive Politics (a name plucked from the land of wishful thinking) 261 members of the US Congress are millionaires, 55 are worth more than $10 million. Congress seemed immune from the economic vagaries of the recession, upping their average wealth from 2008 by 16 percent. Just among the senators, median wealth rose from $2.27 million to $2.38 million. Only a third of Americans favored extending those famous Bush tax breaks for the wealthy. But elected representatives, with some serious money at stake, had their own interests to represent. (Fred Grimm, Miami Herald, Dec 20, 2010)

Elected representatives have shown little interest in fixing America's economic disparities. The top 1 percent of American earners took in 23.5 percent of the nation's pretax income in 2007, up from less than 9 percent in 1976. In 1967, the middle 60 percent of households received over 52 percent of all income. In 1998, it was down to 47 percent. Over the last twenty-five years, more than 90 percent of the total growth in income in the United States went to the top 10 percent earners. The remaining 9 percent of income growth, the leftovers, were divvied up among the lower 90 percent. (Fred Grimm, Miami Herald, Dec 20, 2010)

In 1973, the average U.S. CEO in the United States was paid $27 for every dollar paid to a typical worker. Three years ago, the ratio had ballooned $275 to $1. Michelle Singletary reported in the Washington Post that while the average income for the top one percent of earners rose 281 percent, or $973,000 per household, in the last decade, the bottom fifth saw their incomes increase 16 percent, or $2,400 per household. CEOs are paid more than 350 times that of the average worker.

The growing gap between the haves and the have-nots is responsible for much misery and poverty. Obesity, mental illness, drug and alcohol abuse, homicides, imprisonment rates, lower life expectancy, over consumption of resources, teen pregnancy, and the lack of social mobility all have in common strong links to inequality of wealth.

It is brutal in the market place when considering the volatility of the stock market and everyone doing what they feel is essential to get ahead. It makes me sad and weary when I look around and see so many people not getting it right. It is quite a bit more challenging to survive as a black man in a white man's world. I understand that. Sometimes, we do not notice the drift from the center of the truly important values. The value of the strength and support of black women to the struggle of black men has seen a severe shift from the central focus of black men.

In light of all the trouble in the world, it is critical that black men get their act together and realize the struggles and challenges facing black women today in this God forsaken world.

Black women have always been there for black men. They know the strength, compassion, and wisdom beneath the surface of his dark pigmentation. How long will they have to wait before black men live up to their destiny as leaders and stop succumbing to the weak image created by the larger white society?

As black men continue to flee to the other side, deserting our black women, for women of other races and material gratification, they consume the poison of weakness that other consume in daily rituals of utter decadence. As these so-called learned individuals from supposedly the best schools flee to the other side to also languish in decadence, it is the white flag of the spiritual surrender by which black men give up their women and the future generation of black babies.

The problem I have with wealthy black athletes and the black, educated, elite obsessed with enriching the lives of women of other races is their shallowness and hollowness of spirit. These men, brought to celebrity status by their physical abilities, have fallen short when it comes to keeping their eye on the prize of unity. Caught up in the superficial bubble of prosperity, few speak out against the forces in society that oppress those who are less fortunate. As always, the prevailing attitude is, "I got mine; you get yours."

In our society, we are taught to hoard money. In the process, we forget how to give each other love. Seeing how black men caught up in this malaise of social decadence and how black men are so willing to turn a blind eye to the problems of black women is very disturbing to me.

Hopefully, collectively we can start with prayers and hopes that lead to actualization of a world-changing collective genius born of courage, which to this very day, has not blossomed in American political leadership, in our collective souls, or in our spiritually starved society. The transformation has to first begin within each individual.

It comes down to the pedigree of our souls. Are we materially motivated fluff that pay lip service to virtues, or are we capable of reaching a higher level of virtuous living?

CHAPTER 13

Discovering an Inner Path of Tranquility

Wisdom is a virtuous mind that functions mainly to dispel doubt and confusion by understanding its object thoroughly. Wisdom is not worldly intelligence. It is possible to have great intelligence but little wisdom. For example, people who invent weapons of mass destruction are very clever from a worldly point of view but they have very little wisdom.

Similarly, there are people who know a great number of facts and understand complex technical subjects but have no idea how to maintain a peaceful mind or lead a virtuous life. Wisdom is a special type of understanding that induces peace of mind by clearly distinguishing what is virtuous and what is to be practiced from what is nonvirtuous and should be avoided. Democracy in America appears to be short in its virtuous influence.

We are born to the task of devising wisdom from a realm of disorder. In the form of unhealthy selfishness, disorder relentlessly pervades clarity of purpose and sabotages our ability to know ourselves, real love, and to discover order in life. It is truly disheartening to stumble through the desert of life in search of an oasis, only to find mirages of happiness.

Struggling to survive provides myriad negative possibilities that can destabilize progression toward an orderly existence, tranquility, and happiness. Where disorder ends, happiness begins. The very day we are born, chaos cling to us, as barnacles cling to whales. Chaos is sustained, not realizing that the natural harbingers of conflict and disorder begin with desire grounded in selfishness.

Instead of freeing ourselves from chaos and cultivating intelligence, we maximize opportunities for conflict and disorder in our lives, embracing illusions of happiness through material wealth and powerful sexual cravings. Sensual desire distorts purpose, wastes energy, and blurs vision of life's most poignant realizations. Clarity and truth should be a priority for everyone.

For most black men, entry into this the world, is made under economic duress caused by other seeking to use him and through flawed decision made in search of short-term gratification. Eventually, we all learn, much later in life, and after tremendous mental upheaval, to value self-validation.

Many desperate measures, by black men to overcome uncertainty can be linked to impatience stemming from needs to achieve respect and identity. From hasty choices seeking immediate gratification, black men create his greatest adversities, seemingly out of nowhere. After many trials and tribulations, older and mature black men eventually discover serenity and peace that is not heavily dependent on physical gratification. A tremendous problem for young black men is they do not have access to the wisdom of older black men because in black homes headed by single, black females, the wisdom of a mature male is absent.

When soul-searching about what he is truly up against in society comes home to roost, along comes wisdom and knowledge of environment, self-discovery, inner peace and a deeper appreciation for life. Before discovering this inner path of tranquility based on truth and clarity of what really takes place in society, it is not uncommon for a young black man to feel alienated and victimized by the larger white community.

To overcome adversity, young black men should strive to understand the principles of unity in order to transcend the day-to-day entanglements of the greed-based economy of the larger white community. The objective for black men is to eliminate the fragmented mindset caused by capitalist politics, which creates distortions that are detrimental to spiritual awareness. In this environment, people have a tendency to cultivate selfishness instead of compassion when they are not in touch spiritually with a deep respect for life. Looking within and tempering desires are keys to sustaining inner serenity. Nonspiritual values of material desires and multiple sexual conquests are the antithesis of this peaceful mind-set.

Adversity is manifest as wasted energy spent in pursuit of prestige, power, and domination of others as gateways to sexual pleasure, and drugs that ultimately prevent the development of positive self-awareness. One must negotiate deterrence of self-inflicted pain with great discipline, which is made possible through piercing self-awareness. I say piercing because a new sense of self and purpose must pierce the old armor of tradition. In many ways, we invite adversity to become a life-companion. Respect of life's hardship produces a humble nature. Hardship is one of life's great teachers.

With discipline, I have learned to surf the crest of life's hardship and ride through each corporeal challenge guided by a confident intrinsic peace. I cannot stop appreciating the gift of life simply because life is hard. Not one of us will escape adversity in some form. Maturity develops when each of us actually learns to respect the challenges of our own unique adverse circumstances and take responsibility for our unique challenge without using other's resources through desperate measures or by subjecting women to lies and deceptions for selfish, sexual pleasures.

When I assess the complexity created by lack of personal intimacy, I do so to elevate my level of consciousness above a superficial sense of self. Spiritual underachievement has consistently provided fertile ground for chaos. So, it is extremely important not to complicate or distort knowledge of self and rely on traditional illusions of religion and politics to power my brief journey through the material realm of existence.

While on this journey, one of the best fortifications is to develop a strong internal presence as a foundation. This is possible through an intense knowledge of self. Very few things in life will be threatening after attaining this truly transcendent mode which provides a comfort zone at any level of pain. It is important to know the root cause of each negative situation and to take the attitude that any challenge, however overwhelming, can be discharged. Knowing that you are the creator of your next moment in life becomes the surfboard to ride the waves of hardship that rise relentlessly in the ocean of life.

This transcendent mode of thinking is the first order for each day's battle. We must finding self-instilled acceptance of each moment of each day, while deep within the confines of adversity.

The path of black men contains many adversities and obstacles. Many black men of the entire spectrum of blackness have accepted those challenges and overcome the same personal ignorance that was an impasse for many other black men before confronting similar adversity. Many black men continue to experience obstacles of poverty, racism, growing up without an adequate family structure, and so on. The consummate problem for most black men has been their weakness for sex. It is not easy to discover and maintain clarity and peace while mismanaging hormonal cravings to sedate the pain of inequities in society.

As a young man, it seemed my whole approach to life revolved around satiating powerful sexual cravings. In order to better my life, I had to reconcile desires to mate with more than one woman that conflicted with knowing I should limit myself to just one partner. Life's hardship forces an honest assessment of things that truly matters. The freshness and wholesomeness of honesty leads to a sense of personal fortitude and self-trust. It is up to each of us to construct a solid internal fortress based on honesty that will protects us from deception and unnecessary travail in life. The foundation of that fortress cannot be based on deception of self or anyone else, especially women who are constantly used by men for sex to sedate the pain of not being a whole individual.

Satisfying sexual needs has been particularly damaging for black men who seek to rise above crushing inequities of American society. Women desire more than a superficial acknowledgment of what she physically brings to the relationship. Selfish motives derived of sexual desires and personal insecurity is questionable attributes to build a relationship. Many black men, young and old, are not only guilty but shamelessly present the illusion they will remain faithful just to persuade women, black and white, to sedate them sexually. The black male,s response to the cravings of his libido invariably promotes insensitive undertakings in relationships with the women they profess to love.

Men, in general, are late-bloomers when it comes to understanding that love can and should exist totally independent from physical sex acts. A sexual desire often increases the urgency for a man to enter into a relationship. Many times, men will engage women before they are mentally ready to commit with an understanding of women's need to be loved and not used.

Men's physical need for sex is often confused with feelings of love. This is the first mirage in the psyche of men. Black men find it difficult to understand the difference between true love and physical desire for sex. Such clarity of thought comes with a maturity often forged from experience. Black men should sensitize themselves to motivations for relationships created just to satisfy physical cravings and not put his needs before the needs of women whose lives he will damage through dishonesty and deception. Many mistakes begin in the unprincipled and undisciplined youthful years of black men.

There is also the larger battle of resolving complexities of disrespect between black men and black women. Before those problems can be resolved, black men must resolve their legacy of dishonesty and promiscuity, which often leads to the exploitation and disrespect of the women they profess to love. When this legacy of disrespect has been resolved, the resulting positive energy can be diverted toward building better relationships.

The task of learning how to respect others is very difficult, because, from birth, we've faced the formidable challenge of devising wisdom from a realm of disorder while pursuing pleasure to sedate a sometimes very painful existence. Sedating an unhealthy pursuit of pleasure through the physical senses and organs distorts a clear mind. Without clarity, black men will be deprived of opportunities to advance through educational institutions. At this point, the society in which he lives becomes a hostile environment, providing one setback after another, until he is tangled in snares of trouble beyond his ability to prevail.

Dishonest predatory behaviors hinder healthy developments in relationships between black men and black women. I have analyzed questionable behavior of black men and attempted to relate what approaches can be taken that will help ensure the development of healthy dynamics in relationships based on respectable virtues grounded in honesty. Hopefully black men will learn to respect black women and treat them with respect based on an honest assessment of their motivation to approach her.

Men and women have been traditionally programmed to look outside themselves for a love that should first be cultivated from within. Men, seeking sexual privileges will pay too much in the end when he fails to understand a woman's feelings and needs. Men, in the role of the sexual predator, inevitably end up captured by that which he craves most. Being constantly sidetracked by sensual quests, men lose their moral focus and cease to grow spiritually. It is easy to say this predicament is no one's fault but his own, but fault is a two-way street.

Women take full advantage of the weakness of a man in an equally unethical enterprise. As flawed as her male counterpart, females are also caught in a similar moral dilemma of choosing vice over ethics. Many women contribute to the malaise of dysfunctional relationships from a calculated criterion of love based on material security. This criterion is exemplified in whom and why they choose to mate. Many women choose men alienated within by obsessions of power rather than kindness. Instead of choosing spiritually sensitive men of virtue, women settle for insensitive men who satisfy their material needs.

By the female's positive response to material rather than spiritually and humanistic oriented priorities, men are encouraged to strive for material wealth. Women take advantage of these spiritually weak and sexually motivated men who are blinded by raging hormones. In this sense, women are guilty of encouraging distortion and insensitivity in men by sexually reinforcing shallow virtues with sex. Like her insensitive mate, women are also guilty of not adhering to the dictates of higher virtues. The female's flaws are revealed through the type of men they choose to love. Inevitably, children conceived in relationships, established from dysfunctional choices, are taught to perpetuate the same distorted approach to relationship and life.

Couples prematurely rush into relationships to maintain pace with the escalating costs of survival. Some relationships become means to material ends. It is very important to know oneself before embarking on such an adventure. The word "individual" means a distinctly indivisible entity, not fragmented and divided. A person may be single in the physical sense, but few of us develop the intrinsic strength necessary to live life as a true individual.

A good relationship begins with two individuals harmoniously working with discipline, discerning disorder in their lives and its negative impact on their everyday life. Diversions from truth through pursuits of selfishness and pleasure often cancel good character and lessen one's ability to look out for the better interest of a loved one.

Sacrificing important attributes of self-discipline for physical gratification is analogous to having no sense of purpose in life beyond pleasure. Applying this collective nonsense to our ensuing relationships harms us. We are simply building our lives around our primordial mating instincts.

A supreme love can be discovered if we move beyond the estrangement of loving mechanically in accord with our mating instincts. Loving and living mechanically is the outcome of those who navigate their way through life with blinders on. Loving mechanically creates a spiritual void in us that guarantees failure at developing successful relationships that fosters self-discovery, a natural evolution of wholeness, and psychological well-being of each participant. In time, a relationship with others that is built mechanically will unravel. It is sad, but most relationships pursued by men cater to sexual exploration and are not supported by principles of enduring love.

In unbalanced relationships, when physiological interests subsides and presents a test to the stability of a relationship established without spiritual bonds, the relationship becomes empty, pain bearing, and threatening to the vows of shallow commitments like jagged rocks at low tides. With our neediness exposed, the world seems cold. Many times couples achieve only a physical connection through sex that is construed as love. It has become the norm for couples to accept a lesser paradigm of love, because this paradigm is what they have achieved at a personal level within themselves. In reality, their concepts of love are reduced to hollow mechanical acts of passion.

When analyzed in depth, such attempts at relationships can be deduced to acts born of boredom that we attend to for the rest of our lives. Very few relationships are deeply rooted in truth, because most relationships are nurtured through extrinsic veins dependent on an external source of happiness. The true path of righteousness has roots that run deep into the core of the divine. We simply must grow inward to a profound source of a giving spirituality instead of trusting that one of the external mirages will turn out to be real. Ultimately, the external world is an illusion. The principled, loving spirit within is the true reality.

Many pathways to love are obscured when we continue to value material gratification over spiritual love. In today's competitive environment, people cannot see beyond acquiring worldly possessions and short-term physical gratification.

Despite all the young men dying in senseless wars, rarely are they compelled to sacrifice life and limb to create a truly virtuous and spiritual society. A materially encrusted selfishness contradicts the essence of spiritual goodness required to build a great society. The concessions we make to sacrifice our deeper spirituality for superficial and short-term physical surrogates are more costly than we understand. Bad seeds produce bitter fruit.

The bitter fruit crop of young black men today abandoning black women is a great disappointment. The suffering and struggle by black men should produce fruits of men with sensitivity to the women that struggled alongside him, suffering as he suffered. It is not the women of other races who have his cross to bear. The suffering and struggle has made black men fierce-like gladiators. What woman would not want the power, grace and determination of a man, such as a black man who has prevailed against all odds? The women of other races should not be looked at crossly by black women. Black men, by deserting black women, have lost sight of the prize and should be held accountable for their insensitivity. Martin Luther King Jr. did not envision black women reaching the Promise Land without the love of black men there to complete her dreams of happiness.

Love is quintessentially intrinsic acts of introspection, self-regard, and the opening of compassionate channels from within that inspires healthy respect for all life. Hate, which many consider the opposite of love, spawns from self-conflict, where one becomes lost and lack clarity and purpose. America has come a long way, but people with dark skin are still discriminated against.

We are all young once, and it is exhilarating to surf the extrinsic waves of our passionate youth. However, fringe pleasures of our youth are not meant to last forever. If not discerned properly and placed in check, our youthful mistakes can remain much more prevalent in our adult life. Falling prey to physical desires creates variables in the equation of life that could subject one to unscrupulous manipulation. Relationships based on external beauty and sexual desires are precarious at best.

Trusting and loving someone is the most precarious activity in which we can engage. We must accept responsibility for each other. The lack of inner fortitude is a perpetual roadblock to building solid relationships. Loving conditionally creates an inner void between couples that cannot be filled by superficial love.

A broken device is an appropriate metaphor analogous to many people I know. I can see the manifestation of broken mind-sets in our politics, in the multitudes of differences in our religious beliefs, and in our relationships with each other. The high divorce rate in our society is a testament to the hoards of individuals unable to finish their commitment to each other.

Much pain could be spared if people knew early in their life what it is they are after. With a more profound spiritual focus in life, people can honestly identify the monster in their life and place a check on the drain of their life force. It is very important to know who we are, and it is important to be in touch with the spiritual self beyond the entrapments of materialism.

I have explored the incomplete self as the primary reason people fail to live up to their own expectations and expectations of those they would love. Each time one look for fulfillment outside the individual's means to create it, the person attempts to gain missing parts of the puzzle of who one is from precarious external sources. One should not forsake the inner channels to happiness within. Unfortunately, patterns of seeking external gratification repeats itself like clockwork in today's society, which is transfixed on identifying ourselves through the car we drive or the color of the person we love.

Often pursuing an external concept such as a concretized conceptualization of God, causes one to look infinitely outside oneself. Looking outside for happiness and hoarding material possessions are the basic problems of social progress among men and women and a continual cause of wars and spiritual decay. In cultures where materiality is a measurement of success, quests for material wealth become accepted behavior. Decadence is preceded by collective will fed by greed.

The more one conforms to status quo at society's behest, the less energy there is among the people for spiritual growth. A person can make many regretful decisions when detached from a healthy inner spirit.

Aggression is cultivated in economically challenged individuals. They are less inclined to develop their intrinsic potential, because they have always been in a position of need. They've always been forced to look outside of themselves for sustenance. It is hard to love and be giving when you are deprived of the basic elements of survival.

Aggression is also conditioned in affluent individuals who are molded into takers rather than givers. Conforming to standards of aggressiveness embedded in the activities by gangs, drug dealers, corporate thugs, politicians, judges and presidents in pursuit of gaining or preserving wealth and power compromises the most profound aspects of our spiritual being. We become insensitive to and alienated from our true spiritual nature and cultivate core beliefs of capitalism. After so many years of being victimized by capitalistic institutions, black men have become absorbed in it, just as his flawed white brother.

Beyond life pursuit geared to earning an income in the economic market place, we need to train ourselves in what Sogyal Rampul calls the "ABC" of the mind. The basis of this training is what are called the "three wisdom tools" the wisdom of listening, the wisdom of contemplation and reflection, and the wisdom of meditation. Sogyal Rampul further states,

> Every spiritual tradition has stressed that this human life is unique, and has a potential that ordinarily we hardly even begin to imagine. If we miss the opportunity this life offers us for transforming ourselves, they say, it may well be an extremely long time before we have another. Imagine a blind turtle, roaming the depths of an ocean the size of the universe. Up above floats a wooden ring, tossed to and fro on the waves. Every hundred years the turtle comes, once to the surface. To be born a human being is said by Buddhists to be more difficult than for that turtle to surface accidentally with its head poking through the wooden ring. Even among those who have a human birth, It is said, those who have the great fortune to make a connection with the teachings of enlightenment are rare; and those who really take them to heart and embody them in their actions even rarer, as rare, in fact, "as stars in broad daylight." (The Tibetan Book of Living and Dying)

Despite being conditioned endlessly with illusions of material access as happiness, we must maintain vision through endless streams of illusions of what happiness really is. It is very important to know who we are, and important to be in touch with the spiritual self beyond the entrapments of material value systems. Such control of blocking spiritual awareness is needed in order to keep people enslaved by a cartel of international bankers deluded with powers of grandeur.

Uncontrolled greed perpetuates ignorance, help distort thinking, and leads to making many mistakes, from which it can be difficult to recover. The temptations are many. The fear of not finding fulfillment is never ending, because social conditioning is thorough in leading one to believe happiness is related to material wealth.

Society manifests in a collection of child-like individuals who constantly caves in to the id complex and its demands for more and more sensual and material gratification. We seem to have no clue about life beyond material pursuits. Because of a collective weakness, our society is spiraling out of control.

We see the destruction that such a way of life brings, yet we still cannot bring ourselves to realize that the path we are on is not the path to true happiness. Our lives are reduced to emulating images projected from the movies and television screens. On the other hand, we relish eternal salvation, but we fail to comprehend the necessity to abandon endeavors that serve our insensitive egos.

In a relationship created by two intrinsically oriented individuals, couples find the means that permit each other to explore their individually unique inner sanctum. They align needs and values with a harmonious but completely indigenous love. They love not from a state of deprivation but from an internal resource of plenty. In contrast, extrinsic relationships are more difficult to sustain. Extrinsic relationships are not symbiotic in a positive sense. The extrinsic union tends to be parasitic, whereby one person exploits the other. Often, one party or both are dealing from an internal security deficit, depending on external resources for happiness.

Exploiting others is an easy way to cope with internal pain caused by personal shortcomings. Such relationships are a dime a dozen in Hollywood. Unfortunately for black women when left to their own broken devices, black men have been reduced to a whirlpool of mischief. As the mischief escalates, illusions are embraced as clarity, which makes happiness inaccessible.

Black men and women assail each other never truly understanding the errors of their ways are created by larger society's agenda of racial control that produces the shortcomings, as black men fail to discern a dire reality through smoke screens of confusions created by adhering to distorted virtues, ethics, and principles of the political and religious institutions of the society in which they live.

It is very important to follow the principles and values that are consistent with a sense of inner peace and not the principles of unenlightened and greedy individuals. Black men are guilty of giving up on unique sets of values and have forsaken a virtuous inner journey derived from discipline and virtue. In the flawed pursuits of satiating sexual curiosities in superficial games, sexually conquering black women as well as women of other races, the dream of a deep, abiding happiness at the side of a black man is fast becoming a fantasy for black women.

To prevent such an apocalypse, affluent and successful black men should reinvest in other struggling black men. This would be obvious if the eyes of influential and wealthy black men eyes were on the prize of freedom. Because many eyes are blinded in slumbers of selfishness, millions of people of African descent are dying from HIV/AIDS, and millions are incarcerated as felons. Only affluent black men are able to deliver salvation to the weak, struggling, and under caste black men.

Many pay lip service to a belief in God, many pay lip service to ideas of patriotism, many pay lip service to developing a kinder and gentler nation, and many pay lip service to following values carved from morals and ethics that reflect on our greatest compassions for life. But in the end, the truth is that every person follow the first law of nature: which is self-preservation.

As we operate through belief systems, it is apparent that each of us represents traditional worldviews grandfathered in pride, greed, and, in many cases, myths. Because we do not react to mass incarceration, because we find it difficult to believe the AIDS virus could be manmade, or the middle class permitting Wall Street bankers to rob us blind by not holding politicians accountable for Wall Street's continuing subjugation of the middle class in America to overt thievery, it is clear to me that people are afraid they cannot come up with anything better than the illusion of freedom the Wall Street bankers provide us. It is amazing to witness the unwillingness of the majority to have their views challenged because we would rather believe in things that are unreal, because it is more comfortable.

This is the viral psychosis that black men have become infected with after centuries of being forced-fed empty illusions of freedom and happiness, and hollow practices of ethics and virtues, which construct illusions of justice and democracy and a caste system between the haves and the have-nots.

The greatest viral psychosis passed from white men to black men is the use of religion dogma to control his behavior. Virtues and ethics should be internal in the sense of understanding that one should not hate, instead of following the precept that thou should not kill.

Thou should not hate is a more mature virtue that should be taught. A society ruled by mature virtues requires fewer police, judges, and prisons. For the Greeks, the Roman Stoics, Buddhists, and the Confucians, virtue is its own reward. Christianity instills mechanical responses instead of fostering true love and devotion for one another. We should love, because we should not want another to experience anything we do not want to experience. It is too bad people are motivated by going to heaven in order to treat someone the way they would like to be treated.

References

Rushton, Philippe J. (1996). Race, genetics, and human reproductive strategies; Genetic, Social & General Psychology Monographs,

Cannon, Katie Geneva. The Emergence of Black Feminist Consciousness; Feminist Interpretation of the Bible; Westminster Press Philadelphia

Sanders, Tom (2001). The Double Oppression of Black Women in America; Socialist Action

Hochschild, JL, Weaver; Russell (2007). Remaking America: Democracy and Public Policy in an Age of Inequality; New York Sage Foundation.

Baker, John R. (1981) Race, Oxford University Press, 1974; Athens, GA, Foundation for Human Understanding, 1981.

Siefert, Ruth. War and Rape. Analytical Approaches1

Norment, Lynn (2011). Black Men White Women: What's Behind the New Furor? Ebony. pp 4

Jordan, Winthrop 1968). The Simultaneous Invention of Slavery and Racism White Over Black

Harris, Tamara Winfrey (2010). For Models, Black Beauty Means White Features

Rodgers-Rose, La Frances (1980). The Black Woman. Sage Publication

Robinson, Eugene (2010). Disintergration, The Splintering of Black America. New York: Doubleday

Blassingame, John W. (1977). Slave Testimony Two Centuries of Letters, Speeches, Interviews, and Autobiographies. Baton Rouge: Louisianna State University Press

Laumann, Edward (2004). The Sexual Organization of the City. Chicago: The University of Chicago Press

www.ingramcontent.com/pod-product-compliance
Lightning Source LLC
Chambersburg PA
CBHW020442290526
45785CB00002B/977